# LOVE LESSONS

# Love LESSONS

*Understanding, Learning, and Finding Purpose*
*While Raising Challenging Children*

Jodi Bean

A DEFINITION NOT FOUND IN THE DICTIONARY
*Not leaving:* an act of trust and love, often deciphered by children.
—Markus Zusak *The Book Thief*

*For Victoria,*
The one who has felt
My anger, stronger
My sadness, deeper
My hurt, bigger
My love, courageously

# *Foreword*

BY JAMES DUMESNIL, MS, LPC

A mother's journey.
A child's pain.
A mother's heart being shredded.
A child who thinks she is protecting herself.

Jodi Bean and her husband Jay already had a happy family with three healthy boys.

It is a story heard repeatedly. Great family, great parents, great loving marriage... The family believes it can help others less fortunate. Then... the traumatized child is brought home, and mother's love is tested, challenged, doubted, and put through the fire, like non-traumatized birth children can never do.

*Love Lessons* takes us inside the home, the hearth, and the heart of a family determined to love a child, who has been programmed and conditioned to not accept love and family. The strategies a hurt child can employ for rejecting this love are endless and countless. The pattern is painfully predictable and shared by all. The children create "tests" for the parents to fail. Then the child can remain secure with the belief system, "I knew I would not be loved. I knew it would not work out. I knew I belong alone. I am different. I do not deserve this family, this love, or any family, any love."

*We were at relative's home. Victoria came up to me on the couch and was being very affectionate. This was unusual at this point. Later, when we got into the car, I asked what that was all about. She replied, "I wanted them to think I was nice to you."*

It is hard for most of us to imagine that children can be so destructive and so tormented. But we need to "GET IT!" as a culture, as a people, and certainly as an industry that endeavors to help families and educate children. Children are innocent until…they are not. Once they have been neglected, hurt, and abused, once there have been assaults to developmental progressions, there is really no limit to the amount of damage that can be wrought.

Conscience development can only happen when a child internalizes their mother, father, or primary caregiver. When an infant child suffers "sanctuary trauma" i.e. trauma at the hands of the one who is supposed to keep the child safe, and in the home where the child should find protection and sanctuary, then that child can be expected to be programmed not to trust. The values and belief systems thus internalized, even for a preverbal child, are that adults and the world can not be trusted.

Many of these "children from hard places" are brought home by families who believe they can love the unlovable. They firmly believe their love and their faith can heal the most wounded. Mom and Dad seem to believe, "I can love anyone back to faith in love, and trust in people and God." As the children have the exact opposite programming and core belief, what can follow is sometimes a clash of Olympian proportions. Mrs. Bean brings us inside this struggle. She has the courage and integrity to openly disclose the terror and gut wrenching pain that a mother faces when she starts to "hate" her child. A mother who never knew she could hate a child, much less her own. The self-doubt and self-deprecation that follow are ever so poignant, powerful, and painful.

❧ ❧ ❧

What Mrs. Bean and the best research universities are telling us now, is that there is a path to redemption, even at these lowest moments. What Dr. Foster Cline discovered and taught after decades of working with these families, is that there are two things that make a difference for families that survive and succeed with the child who was traumatized in the beginning: A sense of faith, and a sense of humor. Mrs. Bean is shaken to the very foundations of her faith as she takes the necessary, fiercely, and brutally honest look at her own history. Thank God that her faith was rooted in a secure foundation for she was shaken to her core. Because of this she was able to heal, and to accept herself as people with a strong faith in a loving Creator and Savior are able to do. As Dr. Karyn Purvis has taught, each of us can earn a "healthy, secure attachment pattern." Sometimes a healthy marriage or secure attachment in adolescence and adulthood can help to achieve that. Even with that, many of us need to go back and resolve and grieve the unresolved hurt and trauma from our past. As experience has proven, it takes about six months to two years of a fiercely honest review of our childhood and past. The goal is not to stop at anger, projection, and blame. The goal of this review and self-examination is to keep our eye on developing a sense of forgiveness, and even blessedly a sense of humor about our own history, our family, our first teachers, and theirs. It can be done. It has to be done.

Dr. Karyn Purvis and Dr. Steven Cross of TCU's center for Child Development have developed TBRI, or the Trust Based Relational Intervention. Their research has shown us that most families who typically bring children from hard places home have wounds of their own. Many of these parents are children of alcoholics. Their early programming entailed taking care of those who could not take care of themselves. Not by conscious choice but by unconscious core beliefs, perceptions and programming, they are drawn to take care of those who need help and protection, but who also reject those who dare to try to care of them.

Or, as Jodi Bean's life history elucidates, the "tear" in the fabric of an otherwise healthy secure attachment can be caused by death or divorce. Research on attachment patterns, since the end of WW II, has consistently and repeatedly demonstrated that the infants' attachment patterns at 12 to 18 months of age, will naturally endure, persist, and prevail over the life span. Mrs. Bean's personal experience bears out the research data. Death or divorce of a parent while the child is still young can compromise a healthy secure attachment pattern. Such an experience will be experienced, interpreted, and internalized as a threat to the developing psyche and developing child.

Mrs. Bean repeats often what we nearly universally hear from mother's who take in these children: If only I could have known. If only I would have had the information earlier, a year, five years, a generation earlier...

> *I explained to Victoria that I thought I was prepared to bring her into our family. I wanted her here but when she came, she was mean and angry. "I tried so hard to love you until I became mean and angry. I couldn't figure it out. I didn't know what to do for you and I am sorry."*

Of course to sit in judgment of these mothers and fathers, who have taken in children from very hard places, is smug, irresponsible, damaging, and dim witted, even if it is natural, or human, and almost unavoidable. We all believe we could do better. I think it must be biologically wired into our perception and response systems as people, as adults. We believe that our love, our firmness, our strength, our discipline, or our playfulness could create a different outcome. Mothers like Jodi, constantly hear advice from everyone, including their own mothers; e.g. love her more; be more strict; get him into athletics, activities, etc. We see mother's trying to take the children out in public, in stores, parks, churches, and airports. The children tantrum, and give doe eyes to the unsuspecting. Well intentioned adults fawn and feel sorry for the children. The damage this does at seemingly innocuous or safe settings, such as school and church and family gatherings, is often irreparable.

> *I was getting suspecting looks from the teacher's aide that felt like she needed to provide Victoria with everything it appeared she wasn't*

*getting at home. This was a familiar response to me, even from my own family members. I knew it was difficult to understand from the outside looking in but the suspicion was hurtful.*

*So as hard as it was, for me, it was the right thing to pull her out of the last few months of school. What it simply came down to was this: I couldn't compete with anyone else. I would always lose to the shallowness of attention. Victoria always chose the schoolteacher, the Sunday School teacher, the smiling stranger primarily because they were unsuspecting. She could draw attention out of them and not have to give anything in return. My love was scary to her. My love wanted to give and take. Reciprocity was required.*

As Dr. Purvis and Dr Bruce Perry, and the entire literature on Bonding and Attachment since John Bowlby established the field have demonstrated, the spectrum of parenting that can be successful with bonded and attached birth children can be very broad. Whereas the successful strategies demanded to re-parent traumatized, neglected, and rejected children is incredibly narrow. As one parent, who is a doctor, continued to experience in his struggles with his adopted children often stated, "this is 'Professional Parenting' that is required." And it is. Some would say pragmatic or practical, rather than professional. What these parents seem to mean is that, like a well trained mental health professional, parents cannot take what these children do personally. If a parent gets their feelings hurt by the child, they will likely not be able to survive, much less succeed as a family with these children. If a parent wants or needs to feel loved by their child, they are in a very dangerous place, and What Parent does Not!

Daniel Siegel, MD, and his colleagues have made great contributions to our understanding of Developmental Neuropsychology. Through advances in technology, this research area has been able to demonstrate that theories of attachment are hardwired in brain development. His findings support his conclusion that the "coherent narrative" of the mother, (of the primary bonding figure) is the single greatest factor that determines whether the child will be able to successfully bond and attach to the mother, to the bonding figure. Fonagy from Great Britain have shown that the attachment pattern of an adopted child will mirror that of the adoptive parent after three months of placement.

When children from hard places are taken into the home, what appeared even at deep levels as the "coherent narrative" of the mother and father can be terribly shaken up by these children. The children's trauma history—routinely filled with rejection, trauma, in utero drug and alcohol exposure; exposure to violence, and overcrowded orphanages—is powerful and pervasive. Therefore, their core belief system has concluded: I will not bond. I will not be loved. It is safer to reject, before I am rejected…AGAIN!

Helping birth children make a safe passage from childhood to increasing levels of healthy independence, while remaining attached to family, can give a parent an understandable sense of accomplishment, pride, and a certain security in one's ability as a mother and father. Parenting traumatized, and attachment challenged children will provide the opposite experience of oneself as a parent.

Mothers like Mrs. Bean, who has raised her sons so well, are qualified to bear witness to the fire that burns when a "good home" takes in a child from a "hard place". The courage required of such a journey is unparalleled. She and her husband, Jay, survived and can now tell the story so that mothers, fathers, and professionals anywhere can learn as witness to this journey. And since mothers, fathers, and even professionals are routinely, if not always, heard to say that they need information about this challenge, it is my hope that this can be a resource for adoptive mothers, and those who try to support these families.

Understanding and treating Attachment disorder, Reactive Attachment Disorder, Attachment challenges, or problems resulting from pervasive sanctuary trauma, of the very young, have had a short and controversial history in psychiatry and psychology. Research literature has focused on attachment as a relationship between two people, and they focus on the psychological adjustment of the caregiver. Those in practice, find a struggling family trying to get a child to love them. And the treatment community has tended to place the onus of change on the traumatized child. Thus, treatment and research have often diverged. Universities study the attachment relationship to great gains in understanding. Treatment focuses on attachment disorder as a problem that the "traumatized" child brings to the relationship.

In a way, this different focus for treatment providers is understandable. A loving family, with great morals and values takes a child in. The child rejects the family's love. Is that the family's fault? No it is not. And yet, what experience and perspective are teaching us, is that taking in children from hard places, will often times test a marriage, a relationship, and a parent, to its very core. It is said that adoption of traumatized and attachment challenged children results in an 85 percent divorce rate. This seems believable. If there is a chink in the armor within a parent or within a family, it will be identified, exploited, amplified, and exacerbated by taking these children into one's home. Families, who take these children in need to be understood, supported, and applauded for the challenges they take on for the future of society.

> *I knew it was difficult to understand from the outside looking in but the suspicion was hurtful. Other people thought they could provide what I am not giving. So did I, once upon a time. Just more love. I have loved this girl more than anyone despite what I could not do for her. This love brought her to our home. This love allowed her to stay. This love will mend her. This love will allow her to love others. And despite what they thought, they had not seen her love.*

Should these families be vilified, ridiculed, and unappreciated? Or should these families be seen as the last man on the dike, trying to hold the water back, before it blows for good? Should we be GRATEFUL?

James Heckman, Nobel Prize winner for Economics, 2000, demonstrated that in North America at the year 2000 about 10 percent of our families were high risk families and used up the vast majority of community mental health resources in this country. If current trends in birth rates continue, then by the turn of the century, we will likely have 25 percent of the population at high risk. We cannot support a democracy if one-fourth of the population is at risk. As Dr. Bruce Perry demonstrates, most of our monies spent on "changing" people are spent when children are adolescents and young adults, i.e. once they enter the criminal justice system, and to a lesser extent psychiatric hospitals. If we want to make a difference, then we need to put our resources to work at the beginning of life. Ninety percent of brain development occurs in first three to four years of life. Personality and core beliefs are formed by that age. The attachment patterns observed at 12 to 18 months of age will prevail across the lifespan, barring the untimely death of a parent, or major change in life circumstances, illness, poverty, violence, or addictions while the child is still very young.

Families, who take on damaged, neglected and rejected children, are working for all of us, and for our children's future. As an industry, we simply have to do a better job of preparing families for the challenges routinely inherent in adoption and foster care. As a people and a society, we need to encourage and accommodate any and all willing families who are able to do this work and act of love.

In *Love Lessons,* we do take the intimate journey with Jodi Bean, her husband Jay, her daughter, Victoria, her family, and her therapist, through the challenges and traps inherent in bringing a traumatized child "home" and keeping her home. It is challenging, but both mother and child can be transformed in the process of going through the fire. Mrs. Bean shows us the way in, and the way through. I thank her and everyone around her for making this journey successfully, and furthermore for making it available to the rest of us.

The "wounded healer" is a prevailing archetype of our time. If and when we can honor our path to wholeness with integrity and fierce honesty, love and compassion, faith and humor, we can then help others to do the same on their journey. There is symmetry in balance in coming to the conclusion, that those who can most help the hurt and traumatized children among us, are those who have taken on their own journey, healed their own trauma, and left no stone unturned.

I thank Jodi and Jay for sharing all of the paths and passageways along their journey with Victoria. This is a valuable resource for parents and professionals alike.

# *Prologue*

Dear Victoria,

You are not the daughter I dreamed of. You are my nightmare. You came in and changed and ruined the dynamics of this family with your selfishness. I resent that Noah and I are no longer able to spend time alone while his brothers are at school. I hate that I make excuses for your deliberate and vindictive behaviors. I hate that I allow you to make me so angry I feel out of control. I hate having you here. I can't trust you. I am angry and I blame myself that you needed more love. I feel so much rage and guilt. The anxiety is nearly killing me it seems. I am alone often to take care of you and your brothers. You're taking all of my time being angry. I miss spending time with my boys. I never used to yell at them. They are not used to all the contention you've brought into this house.

I keep making excuses. *Just more time. My expectations are too much.* I take the blame for everything. Nothing can be your fault; you've lived in an orphanage your entire life. I just need to love you more while you take advantage of me.

You push me to the limits of self control. You don't seem to care. I feel the guilt again. You are so intentional. I want to hold you responsible for every indiscretion. You are so sneaky. I spy on you often and my anxiety is nearly out of control. My heart nearly beats out of my chest as I anticipate your next bad behavior.

You are constantly breaking and ripping things up. I don't want to give you anything. I spend hours talking to you. You break promise after promise. Your sincerity is like a sword. I don't know how to discipline you and I hate to be around you.

I am becoming so mean towards you. I hate myself for my reactions to you. No one knows. Everyone thinks you are happy and well-adjusted, but I know you're subtle and crafty. I can't make sense of what is happening to me and I don't care what happens to you. I don't tell you not to swing so high or to slow down or you'll fall. I am angry that I can't figure you out and no one else can see it. I feel crazy. I am anxious because I am so angry. No one on the outside can see the chaos inside. You are sickly sweet to everyone outside the family. You are intentionally annoying to me. You do everything I ask you not to do. You lie about eating candy with the wrappers all around you. Your lies are crazy and your disobedience so deliberate.

I spank you; I yank you; I pull your hair and stick you in the corner. You spit on the walls and pee on the floor. I don't know what to do with you. Many times I've wanted to give you up. But I know this is where you are meant to be. That small, undeniable moment of inspiration when I first saw you allows you to stay and screw up our once peaceful, loving home.

—Mom

Dear Mom,

This wasn't the family I was dreaming about either. In fact, I never dreamt about it. I didn't even know all that was possible for me. I still don't. I don't know what it really means to have a mom and a dad. I don't know what it means for someone to care for me. I don't know how anybody could—or worse—would want to. I don't know anything about really feeling good, doing good, or making good choices. I don't know what it means to love you. I don't even know what it means to love myself. This same wall that is keeping you out is closing me off. It won't allow me feel your love or give you anything back.

You are asking me to do what most kids do naturally and many adults struggle to. You want me to trust in something I cannot see and usually don't feel.

The good in my life never lasts and it was never meant to be lasting. I have lived my life expecting the worst and getting it. Occasionally, I could fight for a moment of happiness. But it requires that I lie, cheat, sneak, and become selfish and controlling. Where is the real happiness in that? I don't know real happiness. How can I believe it will last when I am not even sure it exists?

I came into this family and everyone was so happy. But more than that, everyone was so nice to me. I thought for sure it was because I was doing something to get it. But it didn't stop. I have never felt so good. I have never wished for more. But I don't deserve it and it won't last. You will give me away. I will go back to the place that is so different from here—the place I have always known. I want you to get rid of me now so it won't hurt so badly. I will do everything I can to have you send me away. You will send me away because I have never stayed anywhere very long. You won't want me. My own mother didn't want me.

I can't tell you how I really feel because I don't know what I am feeling. I have always felt this way and I don't know why. You know it as mad and sad. I know it as me.

I knew it wouldn't last. I knew you would begin to be mean and scream at me. That's what always happens. And it happened again. I got you to treat me how I've always been treated. I am not going to love you and I want to go away from here. I feel better knowing that I don't have to feel your love. I feel better knowing you are as mad and sad as me.

—Victoria

# Introduction

When I decided to write this book about my daughter's adoption and first years in our family, I thought I would be writing about Reactive Attachment Disorder (RAD). I thought that sharing my challenges would validate other mothers' complicated feelings. I thought a memoir of my journey would be the kind of book I had wanted to read but couldn't find as I struggled to be the best mother I could to Victoria. *Love Lessons* is about all of those things, but it's more—it's an exploration of the truths that I've learned about myself along the way.

What I have come to realize is the journey from loving to being loved is pretty universal. It is magnified and so tangible in a RAD child but there is a bit of RAD in all of us.

When possible I have taken the liberty to describe things from Victoria's perspective. I noticed in the early days it was easy to get sympathy from others for what Victoria was doing to me. This makes sense. I can voice my torment specifically and fervently. I not only have the words, I can feel them. This small helpless child has only her actions that are speaking louder than words. Unfortunately what she was doing wasn't what she was trying to say. She didn't know how to say it. She didn't know what she was feeling; worse, she didn't know how to feel.

It has taken every ounce of the adult in me, and every bit of the courageous child in her, to mend and heal. I haven't done anything that she wasn't required to do also. This story is really about a mirror. A reflection of me that I see in her. I remember one therapy session when our therapist, Max, told Victoria to look into my eyes and tell me what she saw. "I see me," she said. I smiled. I know she did.

The longer I have her home, the more I understand about RAD, the more I realize how unprepared and naïve I was about the whole adoption process. This book serves three purposes: It allows me to share my story, it raises awareness of the disorder, and for the need for intervention.

My qualifications to write this book are not academic. This is not a resource for scientific explanations of RAD. My intentions are to reveal the emotional trauma and healing both in the bonding figure, me, the mother, and her, the innocent tiny victim of circumstances beyond her control, the neglected abandoned child.

I feel obligated to let you know that I am by no means an expert on attachment disorders, parenting, discipline and (now that I think of it), anything, except my story. This is just one of thousands of stories. No two children are exactly alike and certainly each parent's reaction is different. I am apprehensive to tell my story in print because I don't know if I'll be able to convey the torment Victoria and I endured. I wish, at times, her behaviors were more blatant and obvious. If she were starting fires, killing the neighbor's cat, or being violent it would be much easier for you to see the difficulties, but she is very passive. I suppose she was doing the worst things she could think of in her four, five, or six-year-old world. She didn't need to burn down the house because what she was doing achieved the desired effects.

Her fight to be the person she really is, and my struggle to become the person I knew I could be, convinces me Victoria is here to help me as much as I am here to help her. I know I have taken the road less traveled and as Robert Frost concludes, it really has made all the difference. I may have taken the long road to everywhere, but I see the purpose in each step.

# CHAPTER 1

## *Welcome Home*

*Friends told us how fortunate Victoria was to join our family. I was ready to save this child from a life of neglect.*

On September 5, 2000, Noah, our third son, was born weighing six pounds and eight ounces at 11:47pm in Ogden, Utah.

On September 24, 2000, a world away, our daughter Victoria was born weighing four pounds and three ounces in Minsk, Belarus.

Both children came into this world only weeks apart but under very different circumstances. Noah fell right into my arms. He experienced the consistency and peace that I effortlessly provided. Victoria was placed in an orphanage within months of her birth and fell right through the cracks. She felt the inconsistency and fear of what was not provided. Eight-year-old Noah is content, confident, full of life, with a permanent smile, and love that he freely gives. Eight-year-old Victoria is anxious, insecure, full of fear, hiding behind a beautiful smile, and guarding a heart full of love.

My life before Victoria's arrival could be characterized as simple. I had met my husband, Jay, in Independence, Missouri where I had grown up and when he was visiting from Utah. A temporary summer job turned into something more permanent. A year later, in 1993, we were married. A year and a half later we welcomed home our first son, Cameron. Motherhood was everything I had hoped for. I loved being a mother, caring, nurturing, and encouraging. Cameron is easily identified by his dimples and careful, caring demeanor. He is dependable and logical. He has a quick wit and social personality. I thought I was completely spoiled by my firstborn until two and half years later, in 1997, I welcomed my second son Grant home and realized one could have two amazing, easy, sweet children. Born with red hair, a beautiful fair complexion, and sparkling blue eyes, he enamors everyone with his effortless smile and gentle disposition. Grant is confident, expressive, and daring to be his own person. He is comical and friendly. He fulfils his little brother role but excels in being a big brother to my third son, Noah. Noah fulfills his birthright as "the baby" with textbook accuracy. His personality is strong but compassionate. At first glance he is shy, hiding behind a smile, but he is outgoing, athletic, artistic and smart. He has found a weakness in me and his brothers recognize it and accuse him of being spoiled. I'm afraid they might be right.

But what I'm not afraid of is who my boys are. Each of them is unique but they share a common sensitivity and understanding of others. They are well-behaved and very obedient. I like to think Jay and I had something to do with that but I also believe that Victoria's arrival was made easier by their personalities—a huge blessing in my life.

I had no medical reason to pursue an adoption. In fact, it appears Jay and I had a really good thing going but as soon as I saw that third ultrasound I knew I was done having my own children. Jay and I spoke so effortlessly about it. He agreed that we would be done and any other children, especially a girl, would join our family through adoption. There wasn't a long discussion. We had relatives that had adopted and it seemed perfectly natural to us. So in 2002, two years after Noah's birth, we began our journey to pursue an international adoption.

*Belarus.* I had not even heard of the place before being introduced to it by our adoption agency. It is a small country located between Poland and Russia, north of the Ukraine, part of the former Soviet Republic, and still very dependent on Russia. Their president is considered a dictator by Western standards and the government is constantly being implicated as human rights violators. One rarely finds this country in a travel guide. It is very difficult to acquire a visa because you need to be invited. And besides a humanitarian mission, I'm not sure why you'd want to go there.

Jay and I found our adoption agency, Beam of Hope, in Virginia. It was founded by Michelle, a mother who had adopted from Belarus, and Viktor, who is from Belarus and living in America. They were very successful and instrumental in bringing many children to the United States. They are ethical, open, and well organized. They guided us as we prepared the documents required for our adoption dossier: referrals, background checks, fingerprinting, legal documents, and reports by social workers. We then began the wait for our referral.

A year passed.

While we were waiting, so was our daughter. It was now 2003. Victoria turned three and was moved from the baby orphanage to the preschool orphanage. She has just spent her most critical years of development—without consistent caregivers, with limited nurturing, and with little or no love—in an institution. It is during the first thirty-six months that a child's brain develops and is wired to form emotions and meaningful attachments.

It is the basic trust cycle that develops in infancy. As babies we cry to let others know there is a need. Usually, that need is met promptly, by food, clean diapers, holding, or simply providing relief. In a healthy relationship the cycle is consistent, and from this trust the bonds are formed that we associate with love.

I can't know exactly what happened in Victoria's first four years of life, but I do know it wasn't consistent. How could it be? She had multiple caregivers. Even with the best caregiver-to-child ratio in an orphanage there is no way there's enough time for nurturing or enough of anything.

At this point in my life through raising three boys, I thought I understood this trust cycle. I believed I had the ability to provide this small child with all the love and emotional needs that she had been deprived of. She would come to a nice home, have her own bed, her own clothes, and plenty of food and toys.

Friends told us how fortunate she was to join our family. I was ready to save this child from a life of neglect.

I read books on international adoption and even a few on attachment disorders. I see now, without having experienced life with a RAD child that most of the information in those books was meaningless for me. The information was broad and most did not address the concept of her passive aggressive behavior. I joined message boards and learned about others' journeys to adoption from Belarus. I heard stories of heartache in bringing these children home, but in my limited contact with other adopting parents, it all looked so blissful. They seemed to receive their referral, fall instantly in love with the photo, and live happily ever after. I thought I was well informed. Even after all of my reading, my biggest concerns were Victoria's cognitive development, her physical needs, and speech delays. I was aware of attachment issues, but I certainly wasn't knowledgeable.

Three months before Victoria's arrival home we contacted a renowned international adoption doctor in New York, Dr. Jane Aronson, to review Victoria's files. Dr. Aronson gave her best guess based on the limited medical information provided. She rated Victoria a 3 on the risk scale with 4 being the highest and explained that most of the risk was in her cognitive development.

I am still convinced, despite what I know now, that I did everything I could in preparation for bringing this child into our home.

In May 2004, our adoption agency contacted us with three referrals. I remember getting the VHS tape and excitedly going into the bedroom to see the children. The tapes of each child were less than two minutes long. I watched tiny Victoria struggling to sit up on a chair. She turned around and smiled at the camera, her blue eyes shining. At that moment I felt like she was meant to be my daughter. After the video was over, I offered a small simple prayer asking to know if this was the girl that was meant to complete our family. A warmth enveloped me while a peaceful witness to my mind whispered, "Yes." The answer was intense and undeniable. It had to be because this small moment would allow her to stay in our home. This faith would be *our* saving grace, hers and mine, on my darkest days that lay ahead.

Jay and I anxiously awaited the moment we'd receive our court date. It was nearly all we could talk about or that our friends and family asked us about. Finally, we received word that we would travel in July to meet our daughter and finalize the adoption. We secured babysitters for the boys, visas, all kinds of gifts to take to the orphanage, including bubbles, balloons, treats, and small items for the caregivers. We made the final touches to Victoria's room. Everything was ready and it was time to bring our daughter home.

Jay and I flew from Salt Lake to Amsterdam and then on to Poland. We spent the night in Warsaw before taking a short flight into Minsk, Belarus. There, our translator, Sveta, and our driver met us. Sveta was a wonderful resource and friend as she helped us navigate our way through a foreign land, a different language, strange food, and new experiences.

We stayed at the Hotel Minsk during a time when the President of Libya and other dignitaries were there. We often heard English spoken in the lobby, but there was nothing really relaxing about the place. I always had the strange feeling of being watched, and the coldness of the gray concrete buildings seemed to set the tone for our trip. Here we would also meet our social worker, Natalia, who was professional and kind. They all were very organized and sensitive to our needs and this new adventure.

The next morning after our arrival we set out for the hour-and-a -half drive to the preschool orphanage in Soligorsk. As soon as we left the city limits of Minsk, it was countryside the entire way. We passed small villages, carts being pulled by horses, and people walking and biking in the middle of nowhere. There were farmers in the fields with horses and an occasional tractor. As we drove on the narrow country roads, it didn't take long to see that the dividing lines were only a suggestion. Each time we passed a car, it was a near-death experience as we narrowly missed oncoming traffic in the very narrow lanes.

Our first stop was to meet the Director of Education. As we awaited the Director, a reporter and cameraman entered the room. They told us they were doing a local story on international adoption and asked if they could record us and follow us to the orphanage. We didn't have a problem with that but as I look back I am a bit suspect. It seemed unusual. The Director arrived and interviewed us extensively. She asked us about our lives in America. Why would we want to adopt when we already had three children? We talked briefly about religion and extensively about discipline. We discussed other issues and answered a few questions from the reporter. I didn't know if they were looking for specific answers, but I felt confident in our responses.

We then drove to the orphanage. Turning onto a narrow private lane lined by tall dense pine trees, we finally arrived at an old concrete building with fading paint. The yard was mostly dirt with patches of thin grass and a few playground toys. The director and the doctor met us. Jay and I spoke with them for a moment, exchanging pleasantries and discussing any concerns. The director mentioned with some concern a bump on the inside of Victoria's bottom lip. (After we arrived home we realized the bump was where she constantly chewed the inside of her lip.) They told us that she occasionally wet her bed and rocked to fall asleep because she saw the others kids do it (she continued to do this at home for the first two years). There were no major concerns from the doctor and we had very few questions to ask. Then they left us alone with Sveta while they went to get Victoria. It was during this time that Sveta suggested that we not put Victoria in pull ups or diapers when we returned home. She said we shouldn't give her sippy cups, bottles, or treat her younger than she is and certainly not like a baby. This advice would later be the opposite of everything we did.

As I waited in that stark white office, I was anxious to finally meet this little girl we had been working and waiting for. It felt natural to be there. There wasn't any apprehension, only anticipation.

I heard the tip tap of feet running down the hall and a small, blond, blue-eyed girl burst through the door and ran right into my lap. She immediately called us "Mama" and "Papa". This was about the only thing I could relate to in the books on attachment I had read. Usually secure, attached children approach strangers timidly and cautiously. She wasn't either one of those. But it wasn't enough to cause me any concern. She talked incessantly but we had no idea what she was saying. We took her outside to spend time on the playground equipment and then for a long walk.

Victoria wanted to be held and loved the snacks we brought. She was happy and affectionate. She was so eager. I wasn't expecting this and felt a bit strange in this setting with a new daughter. I was anticipating a much slower period of getting acquainted. I held Victoria's hand as we walked and carried her with her arms tightly around my neck as if we had known each other much longer than the thirty minutes that had transpired. It was a little awkward for me because I sensed she wanted me to respond with the same intensity. Clearly, it was a sign of her inability to understand relationships, especially with me, as a stranger.

We visited Victoria at the orphanage three times. I tried to give Victoria all my attention and smiles. I tried to take in the environment, the other children, and to make sense of conversations, a nearly impossible task since I didn't understand the language. I can look back and see a few things that have more significance now than they did then. Victoria's obsession with my water bottle was an indication of things to come. Upon her arrival home and for nearly two years that followed, she would obsess about drinking anything and in excessive amounts. Her talkative nature and the way she interacted with the other children that had charmed me when we first met, I later realized was very controlling and demanding. The orphans' reactions to her, especially from one little boy, indicated they weren't going to be terribly sad to see her go. I felt the tension between the children when Victoria held a bag of crackers we had given her in her hand. An orphanage worker asked Victoria to share with the children. Victoria's face indicated she wasn't going to share the crackers. A boy sitting near her, with as much contempt evident on his face and in his voice said, "You just take your sweets with your Mama and Papa and go to America." The way she saved her snacks in her pocket was no surprise, but the way she left that orphanage and never looked back, with no tears shed on either side, was. Sadly, it shouldn't have been.

As we continued our visits, we also went to court to finalize the adoption and try to get the ten-day waiting period waived so we could immediately take Victoria home without having to make a second trip from Utah to Minsk and back. The ten days are imposed to give the adoptive parents the opportunity to change their minds about the adoption. The court session was very serious and professional. Our ten days were not waived. Jay wanted to stay and tour Europe. I just wanted to be home. We made arrangements to have Jay return to pick up Victoria alone so we wouldn't have to secure another babysitter for the boys. Plus, I had no desire to return to Belarus. I was just looking forward to getting back to Warsaw, where they seemed light years ahead of Minsk.

Jay traveled back to Belarus to bring Victoria home. She would be one of the last children adopted out of Belarus; on October 4, 2004, they closed their borders to most international adoptions pending new regulations on their adoptions laws. The government is trying to encourage in-country adoptions, but the closure has more to do with tension with the United States government. So children are waiting at the mercy of political discord.

I was relieved to be home with my boys but I won't ever forget the experience of being in an orphanage in a small remote village in Eastern Europe. While the dwellings were old and simple they were clean and accommodating. It isn't the structure that haunts me, it's the children's eyes. Most of them had a yearning and a few had distant stares. Now that I understand the cost of abandonment and neglect, I pray they find relief and healing. It's a price my boys will never have to pay but they too are beginning to understand the cost.

When Jay and Victoria finally arrived home, she stayed very close to Jay. I didn't even attempt to put myself in her shoes or try to see things through her eyes. I just thought an abundance of physical and emotional affection would be enough. I thought if she was scared, worried, or sad she would show it. She never did. Looking back she must have been frightened. First of all, she was with a man. She had spent her entire life surrounded by women caretakers. He could not speak her language. Victoria couldn't tell him she was fearful or uncertain. They rode on trains and planes. I don't even know how often she had been in a car.

From Jay:

*Traveling to Belarus for the second time to pick up Victoria was an interesting experience. It was also my first experience with a daughter. When I arrived at the orphanage to pick her up, the workers just stripped her down and gave me a naked little girl. I wasn't sure what I was supposed to do. I felt uncomfortable with this little girl and pile of clothes. The workers eventually dressed her in the clothes I had brought and Victoria ran out of the orphanage. No goodbyes to the children and a very brief goodbye to the caregivers.*

*In the van she ran back and forth between the back and the front looking out all the windows. I was surprised she didn't look frightened. She never did. I would take her to the park in a stroller. I took her to McDonalds and she didn't like ice cream, but she did eat french fries off the ground.*

*I didn't learn any Russian before I went. All I had was a list of words spelled phonetically that Jodi had given me. On the first night in the hotel, Victoria woke up screaming. It reminded me of someone having a night terror. She had peed in her bed and was standing in the middle of the floor. I tried to put her on the toilet as she was kicking and screaming. I had to hold her hand as she sat there.*

*The following night we took the train to Warsaw, Poland to get our visas from the US Embassy. She ate and slept well but she did poop in the bathtub and all over the toilet. So while she never looked scared, she must have been terrified.*

*It was exciting to bring her home. She was charming on the air-*

*plane getting the attention of everyone around us. She wanted to use the bathroom on the plane all the time. When we got home everything was exciting and new. It was a bit confusing with the language. She still didn't seem to be afraid of anything. She would jump into the pool although she couldn't swim. She wasn't afraid of people. There were odd behaviors. She answered the front door naked one day. She devoured hot sauce at a Mexican restaurant. She didn't seem to have any feeling.*

Cameron, Grant, and Noah were excited to see her. There were plenty of smiles and hugs. The boys had been supportive of the idea of bringing a sister into our home from the moment we mentioned it to them. They were sensitive to her and liked to carry her around the house. At four, she was about the size of a two-year-old.

For the first few months Victoria appeared to be happy. She was affectionate. She loved to be held by anyone and everyone. It was this alone that convinced me she was in no danger of not attaching. Our little girl was receiving so much attention in the first six months, it was easy for me to overlook any serious signs of an attachment disorder. In fact, there was no way I could have identified those signs because I had no idea what they looked like.

We had fun seeing Victoria enjoy her first everything. She didn't like ice cream initially. It was entirely too cold for her. She loved familiar foods like rye bread, cucumbers, soup, chicken, and especially fruit. Her favorite was bananas. I can still hear her saying it with an accent. I remember our first visit to the grocery store. I pushed Victoria around in the cart and she pointed to everything. As I put food in the cart, I didn't understand a word she was saying but noticed she couldn't contain her excitement. As we got to the checkout stand and I began to put the food on the counter she freaked out. She began screaming and pointing at the food. She thought I was giving it all back.

By her third month home Victoria could understand nearly everything we said. I put her in the school district's preschool speech program where she did very well. By the sixth month, she was putting a few words together. Her first phrase was "Come eat!" She would say it to her brothers at all times of the day, even when it wasn't time to come eat. It was cute and I know she loved the reaction she got when she saw them all running to the kitchen. Her associations with food, as a child raised in an orphanage, were not lost on me. After a year with us Victoria was speaking in full sentences with no accent. I am not certain, but I don't think her Russian language skills were very well developed.

I spent much of my days being purposeful and loving towards my daughter. I would cuddle her in the mornings when she woke up. I would read simple Russian and English books to her. I spent time carefully dressing her and doing her hair. I painted her nails. Our most intimate times were in the evenings when I would hold and rock her. She followed me around everywhere. I can still see her walking right behind me while I mowed the lawn.

Victoria never looked uncertain. I couldn't have comforted her in the ways that she needed because I couldn't see any fear. For the next four years she wore a smile on her face no matter what she felt. Mostly because she didn't know what she felt.

At first our little girl blended in so well with our family. She fit right in and I was amazed at the transition. I will say I experienced some unexpected mourning for Noah because we had spent so much time together before Victoria arrived, but the transition didn't seem to hurt our relationship.

I expected some problems with the language barrier, potty training, eating new foods, and going to strangers. But after about three months, more complicated things began to manifest. They were subtle and unspoken and made me feel very uncertain about myself and confused. Victoria was sneaky and suspicious. She seemed deliberately difficult. She constantly did things I asked her not to do. She either wouldn't do things or did them wrong. When she would finally obey she was slow and controlling, but on the outside she looked happy, outgoing, loving, and friendly.

If Victoria had been able to write down her experiences, they might have been something like this:

They tell me I am going to a new home. This will be my fourth home and I am three years old. I am going to have a Mama and a Papa. I don't know what that means but everyone is excited. I already have three mamas here. I will have a family, but I have to go to a place far away from here. They tell me when they speak, I won't understand what they are saying. I am so lucky to be going to America. Why am I lucky? I remind all the kids I am going to America. It makes them jealous. It makes me feel better.

I live with 12 other children. We do the same things everyday. We get up and make our beds perfectly. I have three pieces of clothing in my locker and my sandals are too small for my feet. And it is the same for everyone else. I carefully put my clothes away. I don't want to get into trouble. But sometimes I do. Sometimes I want to be noticed more.

We eat at a large round table and our drinks are in the middle. We can't have them until we have eaten our food. I want to drink it first and then I want more. We don't get more and we can't ask. All the kids here want more of everything. I am jealous when someone gets more something I don't get. But if I get more, I am happy. I don't want to share it. There is not enough.

My mamas are always too busy. I don't try to feel bad or sad. It doesn't matter. They don't have time for me. I just pretend to be happy. Happier than the other kids so they don't think anything is bothering me. If something is bothering me, they can't help me.

They are making a video of me today. They give me a dress I have never worn. I like it. But I won't wear it again. They fix my hair and put a bow in it. I like it. But I won't wear it again. They are being very nice to me. We never get candy. Today I am special because they are giving me lots of candy. It makes me feel happy. I like to get things. That is when I know they like me.

They don't give me things very often so I try to get other things from them. Sometimes it is a smile; sometimes it's a slap. Sometimes it is a short glance; sometimes it's a mean glare. It doesn't matter to me. I have to try hard to get them to do any of this. I am pretty good at it because I am always thinking about it. I feel nervous because I am not sure what I am going to get. It is mostly bad. But I have to be fine with this smile on my face.

I sleep with twelve other kids in the same room. We each have our own bed, a blanket and a pillow. The boy next to me likes to push me off my bed at night. It hurts me. I cannot tell anyone because we should be asleep. I rock to get to sleep. I like the way it moves my head so fast, I cannot think very well. I don't know why I do it but other kids do it too. When I wake up, if I am mad, I will pee in my bed. Mama does not like this. She gets very angry. I have to take care of my bedding and my clothes. I don't like that part.

We don't have very many toys. We break the ones that we have. We play outside sometimes. My favorite thing to do is swing. I love the movement in my body. It reminds me of rocking. Some kids know it is my favorite thing to do and they will get on the swing first and won't let me on. I try to find something they want and I won't give it to them.

We go on walks. I hate walking. My legs are so tired when we go but we get to eat tiny strawberries. They make my fingers all red and we eat so many they have to make us stop. Sometimes I get home and my stomach hurts but it doesn't matter. When we go on a walk again I will still eat as many as I can.

Did I tell you we can't ask for anything? But I try. I don't get it. I am really thirsty but I can't have a drink. Sometimes I ask for a drink and I am not thirsty. I think one time they will give it to me.

I like it when the Mamas and Papas come to pick up the kids.

They bring us fruit. It is a really big box but I only get a tiny piece. But it tastes so good. They bring us treats I have never tasted and games I have never played. I think they like the clothes I have on or the way I look at them nicely so they give me these things. I also like it when they come because we eat good food and the Mamas are so nice on that day.

My Mama and Papa are coming soon. My mamas tell me I must be happy or they will not take me. They tell me I must eat my food nicely or they won't take me. I will do all of this so they will want me. But where are they taking me? I don't like not knowing.

My Mama and Papa came today. They seem very nice. We don't understand each other but they bring lots of treats and toys. I take my Mama's water bottle and drink all the water. I wish she had more. They hold me, carry me, push me on the swing and follow me everywhere. This is fun but I wonder if they will come back in the morning.

They do come back in the morning. They bring more food and treats. They also bring balloons for all the kids to play with. I have fish crackers and they tell me to share. I don't want to. A little boy tells me to take my sweets and just go to America. He is jealous. I am happy.

# CHAPTER 2

# *Pushing Away For Control And Comfort*

*I am tired of Victoria being so good around others and so conditional around me. It makes me feel crazy.*

*I* can now admit that the glasses I was looking through were a wee bit rosy. There are myriad reasons people choose to adopt. A universal reason is that of service. I knew that I was capable of providing Victoria with all the material and emotional needs that she had lacked for many years. She had her own room, her own bed, plenty of food, clothes and shoes that fit, and most importantly, love. I believed it would make all the difference in her life. Yet, it didn't. I wasn't as prepared as I thought. I don't know what could have qualified me for this. I certainly didn't have difficult boys, so I was completely naïve and ignorant about how to handle controlling and manipulative behavior. What Victoria did, and how she did it, was behavior I didn't even know was possible in such a young child.

After a brief honeymoon period, Victoria began pushing my patience with her need for control. I started to notice some consistent behaviors that I could no longer attribute to a language barrier. At the time they seemed insignificant, so I didn't recognize there was a problem. Her disobedience was not blatant. It was tactical and subtle.

I remember specifically trying to teach her colors. She was so eager to learn and seemed to grasp information quickly; except when she didn't. I couldn't understand why when I was holding four crayons she could get the colors right but when I only used two she would get them wrong. She did this with many things. She would act like she didn't know how to do something that I was convinced she did. But I couldn't just ask her "Why?"

39

I spent too many hours asking her that question. I really thought she knew the answer to the question of "Why?" For the most part, she didn't. Most of it had to do with her being controlling and my frustration was the sign she needed to gain that control. The following letter explores this from my sister Jaclyn's perspective:

*Last summer when we came to visit, Mom tried to prepare me for how you and Jay were disciplining and so forth. It didn't sound all that bad and I really didn't think much of it. By the second day, I told Roger [her husband] I didn't think I could stay the whole week watching the way Victoria was being treated. You sat down with me and explained everything to me. I then had a little understanding of what was going on and could bear watching Victoria with her struggles.*

*I came out to stay with you for two weeks last December, which still only gave me a little insight into what you deal with on a daily basis. I could see a difference with Victoria when you were around and when you weren't. She would definitely try to get away with things with me and sometimes she would if I wasn't paying attention. For example, when I fixed her lunch she would ask me for a specific drink or something different to eat and not thinking I would say 'okay' and get it for her. However, I remembered your instructions about not letting her choose and make the choice for her and realized that she had pulled a fast one on me. So the next time I made sure I had her food and drink ready for her before she sat down and when she realized I wasn't going to let that happen again then she didn't challenge me. She came home from school and started on her homework. When I checked it she had some letters backwards. I went over it with her and explained to her what she needed to fix. I came back to check it and there were still some wrong answers. I kept working with her and being so nice with her. You and Jay told me that she knew how to write her letters and that she was doing it on purpose. I felt dumb that she had worked it again, getting more attention from me. So the next time I just left the answers wrong and didn't have her fix anything. And of course when we were in the car she would talk and talk even after being asked not to and would fight with Noah and so forth. I just ignored her and asked Jay if he had a chore for her when we got home. She will definitely try to get everything out of someone that doesn't know her. It seems once you know what to expect and are consistent, then she doesn't try the boundary lines anymore.*

*You didn't want her to sleep in the same room with me, but I insisted that it was not a problem; however, I should have trusted your reasoning because you know her better than anyone else. The few nights she slept in the same room, I felt very uncomfortable for some reason. I don't even know why. I thought I would open my eyes and see her standing right there over me. It was a little freaky and I can't even explain why because she never did anything to me to make me feel that way.*

*—Jaclyn*

I enrolled Victoria in dance class. I could not bear to stay and watch. She was unkind to the other girls. She would irritate them when the teacher wasn't looking, cut in front of them in line and constantly demand her teacher's attention for things she knew how to do. It was subtle and the teacher didn't pick up on it. Or at least she never said anything to me. I could tell Victoria was anxious and unfocused. I eventually withdrew her from dance and a year later enrolled her in gymnastics. The behavior repeated. She hung all over the instructor asking for help. He picked up on it and would call her on it saying, "Victoria, I know you know how to do this." She would insist that she didn't. I eventually took her out of gymnastics also.

I noticed very early that Victoria struggled to make choices. Not just good choices but anything. Asking her if she wanted an apple or an orange was tormenting. She didn't think, "I'll choose the apple and have an apple." She thought, "If I get the apple, I won't get the orange."

*Even when it appeared she was doing absolutely nothing it was draining because she was always doing something. Her mind was constantly engaged trying to stay in control and stealing the attention that accompanies that need for control.*

In the early years Victoria wouldn't go to sleep. She would get out of her bed. When she finally stayed in bed, she would force herself to stay awake for hours. Victoria would rock herself, which is typical behavior of children in an orphanage. The bi-lateral movement, or any repetitive movement, releases serotonin and is an attempt to self-soothe and self-regulate. Therapists recommend that when children begin to rock, you should cuddle with them to encourage them to stop. Victoria's rocking never looked soothing but I guess it was. She would rock lying down going side to side with her arms outstretched and hands clasped together. This was not slow and gentle, it was fast and furious. So whenever I saw her rocking, I would cuddle with her. This cuddling was purposeful and intense. I wanted her to find comfort in me. I would hold her close, gaze into her eyes, sing her songs, tell her stories, or gently touch her face. I spent hours doing this. I thought I was finally allowing her to feel a mother's love. I was scaring the hell out of her. Or at least adding to all the fear that was consuming her. This little girl never looked scared. Ever. The love Victoria was feeling from me in those cuddling moments was frightening because it was a feeling she had never before experienced. These were feelings she had never encountered before. They felt too good. They felt like they wouldn't last. It felt like she wasn't worthy of it. It felt vulnerable. I couldn't have known all these things, but I did know that despite the smile Victoria had on her face, her eyes seemed empty. So as time went on, the rocking became less about comfort because she wouldn't allow it to be comforting. It became more about attention. She could control the rocking if she wanted to and it became a power struggle in which she won both ways, either by pushing me to frustration or superficially taking my caring, but never allowing it to form a bond.

Toilet training. I anticipated some delays but encountered so much more. In the beginning Victoria had "accidents" often. Early on I was sensitive to it. She was in new surroundings with strange and different toilets. The flushing noise of the toilets scared her. She wore pull-ups for the first year she was home, but as time went on it didn't get better, it got worse. It didn't seem accidental. It seemed intentional. So we limited her drinks at night (as you will see later, this seemingly simple act became a nightmare), made sure she went to the bathroom before bed, and occasionally woke her up in the middle of the night to use the bathroom. None of these approaches worked. From a doctor's recommendation, when Victoria said she needed to go during the day, I would delay her. This delay was to strengthen what might have been weak bladder muscles. So when she would tell me she needed to go to the bathroom, I would try to distract her by giving her something to do or entertain her for a while, but then, she needed to go to the bathroom ALL of the time. Initially, I didn't realize Victoria was doing it for the attention. The only thing I picked up on was how irritating it was. When I wouldn't entertain her, she just stood there and peed in her pants. I remember in the mornings, I would wake up and the stress would over-whelm me just thinking about walking up the stairs to her room. I knew she would be wide awake rocking violently as soon as she heard the door-knob turn and have just peed in bed. She would be soaked from her head to her toes or only her pillow would be wet. It seemed controlled and stra-tegic. She would look at me with forced innocence and a smile that screamed, "I got you!" and she had.

We tried positive reinforcement. I would give her praise, stickers, or treats. I didn't know rewarding RAD children with praise, stickers, or treats wouldn't work. They don't feel worthy of it and it just sets them up for failure. They know they won't be able to maintain the obedience. It is too much pressure.

If Victoria stayed dry for a while, I would make a "big deal" about big girl underwear, and she would pee in them every single time. She would walk right to her bathroom door and stop and pee on the floor, in her car seat, or while standing in the garage. This behavior had everything to do with demanding attention and exerting control, which fueled my mad-ness. Finally, in my inability to make sense of it all, I had to ignore it or respond to her calmly. I had to act as if it didn't bother me and had her scrub her clothes, the bed, or the floor. This was what it took for Victoria to finally stop but the self-control required to ignore a child that seemed to be peeing out of malice was exhausting.

Victoria did everything so slowly, especially eating. The natural consequence would be to take her food away after about fifteen minutes. However the rage that ensued was so intense. She would scream, kick, pull on her hair, or throw things. I remember feeding her to avoid the rage but that only catered to her need for attention. Then, to exert some control, she wouldn't swallow. I would react by trying to force her. Fighting her for control only enraged both of us, and that was her goal. Eventually she was so successful that I had to put a time limit on her eating and just deal with the rage. Yet, she still asserted control because then it became a matter of eating everything she could. She would even eat things that shouldn't taste good. I remember being completely confused by this behavior. I once put vinegar on her cereal instead of milk to see if she would eat it. She did. It was through moments like this I knew something was seriously wrong. After four years she got to the point where she would actually say something didn't taste good but she still struggled to control her portions. She would eat as much as she could get. It was sad because I felt like she was relying on food to make her feel good and it was never enough. It wouldn't ever be enough.

It was the same with liquids when she first arrived. Victoria's obsessions with drinks was maddening and confusing for at least a year, maybe two. She wanted as many drinks as she could get and would drink all of them. I think Victoria was also trying to feel a sense of *enough*. Telling her she could not have drinks after seven at night only encouraged her to do everything she could to find a drink and lots of it. She would sneak out of bed and find a drink anywhere—the sink, the tub, the kitchen, and even the toilet. Incredible. At church, friends' houses, a cup sitting on bleachers at a baseball game—everywhere. She had a one-track mind. The more fluids, the better. I wish I could say I suspected other motivating factors, but I simply didn't. After responding with patience that progressed to anger, I had to find it in me to ignore her demands. It was difficult for me to help Victoria work through these food issues because I felt so much competition with her dependency on food instead of me.

Victoria's lying was incessant and crazy. For example, I would ask her to play in the playroom. When I would walk up the stairs, she would be running from her brother's room into the playroom. I couldn't even ask her what she was doing. She would lie to the death even if we made eye contact as she ran from his room. She would lie about eating candy with the wrappers all around her. I spent far too many hours trying to get the truth out of her. It would drive me to a rage.

This little girl was so fearful of the truth. She didn't even know what the truth was. She just wanted me to be a reflection of her. And I was beginning to be.

Destructive. I had no idea what these actions really meant. Victoria didn't value anything. Why would she? Not only had she never had anything of her own to value, she didn't even find any value in herself. She would destroy toys, her clothes, furniture, and things (that after three boys) I thought were indestructible, such as a metal baby stroller. This made me not want to give her anything. Again, it all looked so intentional. Eventually when she couldn't find something else to destroy, she became destructive to herself. She would pick scabs, bite her lips and fingers until they bled, pull on hangnails, or pull out her hair. She always had bruises up and down her lower legs. This was a direct result of the intense anger she harbored toward herself.

Victoria was always sneaking. Sneaking food, toys, and drinks—anything forbidden. This was a recurring theme in my life that took me far too long to pick up on: the more I told her not to do something the more she did it. Being sneaky is still her defiance of choice, particularly in stealing food from the pantry. It isn't as much about the food as it may have been in the beginning. She knows there is enough now, but stealing feels good to her. She likes the adrenaline rush she gets from successfully stealing but also experiences some kind of satisfaction when she knows I am aware of it. If it wasn't stealing, it would be something else. And I didn't want to find out what.

Talking. You couldn't hold an intelligent conversation with Victoria. I still struggle to now, but in the beginning her talking was simply incessant and mindless chatter. She would speak in incomplete sentences, pose endless questions, or constantly interrupt and, of course, asking her to stop was like pouring gasoline on a fire. Most of the time this would happen in the car when I had the least amount of control. If I stopped the car and asked her to quit or yelled at her, she gained control and she knew I had no idea what to do. Victoria experienced satisfaction both ways.

I would ask her to get dressed and she would put her clothes on inside out or backwards. She would put her shoes on the wrong feet or wear two different shoes. She would suck on her clothes, rip off buttons, and cut holes in her jeans. During these first two years, every little intentional and annoying behavior got a reaction out of me. I had no idea where she was coming from. And there were so many more subtle behaviors in which she exerted control, but above and beyond that, her physical aggression included hitting, spitting, biting, pinching, and kicking.

I have often spoken to my boys about Victoria's actions during these first few years of having her home. They all remember her defiance. Cameron talks about her annoying behavior and how he was embarrassed by her. Grant thought she would be nicer and struggled to have patience with her. And Noah said she was hard to play with and he will admit that during the first couple of years he hated her. Next to me, Noah had the most interaction with Victoria. He was on the receiving end of much of her subtle abuse, which included lying, sneaking, playing unfairly, and being demanding. I can look back and see frustration and anger from him that probably came from their relationship, but the boys mostly remember my anger. I really do think I, on a subconscious level, did everything I could to protect them from Victoria's abuse. And while I still don't fully know what impact she has had on them, I have tried to be open and honest with them in helping them try to understand her behaviors. I have also taken them to therapists to help them talk through their feelings about Victoria.

I know I didn't protect them from my anger. The change in me was what I have always felt was most destructive to my sons. I realized I was becoming a mother they never knew. I saw the fear and uncertainty in their eyes, but when it came to Victoria, the worst part for me, the part that broke my heart and spirit to the core, was her lack of remorse for it all. I was trying so hard to nurture and care for her emotionally despite what, I didn't know at the time, were her control and survival techniques. I could not, in my limited knowledge, even begin to suspect that she didn't have a conscience. But on some level I sensed it. She simply didn't care. How was *I* supposed to keep caring?

I can tell you this: while I couldn't make sense of her behaviors, I was certain that something was terribly wrong. I knew this little girl was exhibiting normal negative behaviors in a very dysfunctional way because it all seemed so very purposeful and calculated. Victoria quickly learned the behaviors that set me off, and she was relentless. I was uncomfortable leaving her alone, and when I was with her, I always felt like her mind was actively scheming to maintain control over me.

As I shared these and other behaviors with family and friends, I always got the same response. "Lying? Sneaking? Oh, my kid does that." Or "Talking? Wetting the bed? That's a girl thing." And even, "You finally got a difficult child." A favorite was, "Well, if she was in the orphanage for four years, you need to give her four years to adjust." These were all statements from certainly well intentioned, caring people that did nothing to help my situation. Never once did I hear something that could explain the lack of love I was beginning to have for this child. That was scary for this mother whose natural instincts are to be so nurturing. Those natural tendencies were running for the nearest exit!

After Victoria's first year with us, I began to believe I was crazy. I had no one that could witness, feel, or understand what her behaviors were doing to me. Jay traveled most of the first two years Victoria was home. He was gone about two weeks of each month. When he was home, he knew she was annoying, challenging, and deceitful, but she would behave differently around him. He accepted her charm and she recognized that acceptance but he was also all about justice. I couldn't do that. I had to try to temper my justice with mercy but I had a heart that wouldn't allow me to do it.

Victoria would often wait until I came into the room to set me up for her disobedience. She looked suspicious and I picked up on it. I soon found myself watching her every move. It came to the point that I was consumed with holding her responsible for every act of disobedience and she became paranoid. I became paranoid. We were both operating on *very* high levels of anxiety. I was on edge, experiencing anxiety attacks (I recognize that now), yelling at the other kids, becoming depressed and so very confused about what exactly she sought. She wanted me to feel like her. This little girl didn't know why she felt that way and neither did I. This was not "like my child" or "a girl thing" or "a typical difficult child." I have learned she was a textbook example of a passive-aggressive child with an attachment disorder and so were my destructive reactions.

The stress and anxiety I felt from her demands and my lack of understanding were beginning to push me to the edge of sanity. And it was intensified by her behavior outside of our house. If you did not live with her, this is what you saw: beautiful, happy, obedient, always smiling, sweet, charming, extremely smart. If you lived with this girl, this is what you saw: fear, anger, vengeance, manipulation, misery, beautiful, extremely smart. This alone made me feel completely crazy. Literally, I could not make sense of the world I was living in and worse I couldn't explain it to anyone else. Even now, my husband, Jay (who now understands her), cannot comprehend the intensity of the early days. These RAD children typically save their most destructive behaviors for the mother because that's where they feel the most love and hence the most loss of control, which threatens them. I knew others believed I just had a strong-willed, difficult child, but it was so much more complicated than that. I was starting to convince myself that I was the problem, but all of these seemingly normal difficult behaviors were coming from a very destructive place. I couldn't make sense of it, but I felt it deeply. And unfortunately, I was reacting to all of it.

I felt inadequate. Conditional. Unfair. Angry. Misunderstood. We were treating her so differently from the boys and I didn't like it. But Victoria *was* so different. There was no trust, no sincerity, and no real emotion. I was living with a plastic flower. She looked perfect but there was no feeling. But again, unless you lived with her, you couldn't see it. So I felt an enormous amount of guilt projected by those on the outside looking in. The misunderstanding and contempt I received from others (and sometimes still do) was painful and discouraging. I so often heard, "She just needs more love," or "You need to show her more physical affection." And to the outside observer that's exactly what it looked like. For me, not only had I tried that with no results, I was in a place where even if that would have helped, I was depleted. The problem for parents is that, to everyone else, many RAD children appear so normal. Outsiders only see are a few annoying behaviors and over-reacting parents. But what these stressed-out anxious parents are trying to do is respond to what most people can't see: children who don't trust, push away their best efforts, feel entitled and deserving, always looking for attention and are quick to anger. Even Victoria's smile and feigned happy disposition made us appear all the more unreasonable.

I had virtually no patience with her and found myself yelling at all the kids. For me this was so disappointing because it meant I was out of control. I realize now it was more than a lack of control, I was suffering from Post Traumatic Stress Disorder (PTSD) as she was systematically targeting all of my weaknesses and trauma. It is this condition that also makes it difficult for me to remember many specific interactions with Victoria during the first two years at home. I had always been self reliant and strong. My inability to cope was causing me to lose my ability to regulate my emotions and scaring me because I couldn't find the strength to manage them (RAD children suffer this same fate from their trauma and bring it into their new homes). While I didn't realize I was experiencing PTSD, I can remember on many occasions the feeling of that trauma beginning in my feet and rising throughout my body and seizing it. I felt frozen. I could only react to protect myself. I recall one night specifically when Jay was out of town. It was the end of the day and while I can't remember the specifics of what transpired, I can still remember the atmosphere and the recklessness. I know Victoria was being defiant. The boys also wouldn't clean up and get ready for bed. What occurred next was more than a parent's usual frustration and impatience. It was more than just yelling, it was being physical. I remember grabbing the boys, strong-arming them, and pushing them into their rooms. The panic in their eyes told me they were looking at a stranger. I then went and unleashed my fury on Victoria spanking her hard. I remember three times. *SLAP! SLAP! SLAP!* And if anyone wondered what I had done they could just look down and see my handprints to prove my guilt. There were a few other times when I knew I was spiraling downward.

I was taking much of the blame for her actions. I clearly needed help but I didn't know who could help. I didn't know where to go for help. I couldn't even really explain what the problem was. For far too long I believed I was the source of the problem. Nobody would think that this small girl could cause so much torment. I could hardly accept it myself. The dynamics of my family were in turmoil. The spirit in the house was contentious. I was in a constant state of hyper-vigilance, with a rapid heartbeat, nervousness, and panic; and I had no outlet. All the while, I tried to put on my best face publicly. I felt like a fraud. No one around me knew what was happening to me or inside our home. I was becoming and doing things I had told myself I would never do as a parent. It was causing the trauma I was feeling from her to be more intense than it ever should have been. These feelings, in varying degrees, lasted for over two years.

I constantly beat myself up for expecting so much from Victoria, but I was so confused! Sometimes she would live up to my expectations and at other times it turned into a battle. I would expect less from her but that also came across as controlling. By the time I realized that her need for control would never subside, by the time I realized her sincerity was all an act, by the time I realized she saved her worst self for me, ignoring her behavior was out of the question. I demanded justice. I thought I could "make" her experience remorse for her actions. But there was nothing. No amount of punishment, no matter what kind, changed Victoria's behavior.

What I did know was this: for all her wrong decisions and negative behavior, there needed to be consequences. How should I discipline this behavior that seemed (to the outside observer) to be unintentional or accidental? I drew on my limited discipline techniques that I'd used for three very obedient boys. We began with a time-out. Victoria would stay in time-out and never try to leave, but she would turn around and smile at me, spit on the wall, or pee on the floor. Many times she would blow snot out her nose wiping it all over herself and anything around her. Again, exerting control. I could not withhold things from her because she didn't value anything, although she acted like the very thing we were taking away was life itself. She would scream and cry the instant we took a toy away, but she didn't care if she ever got it back. Her reaction was superficial. And as time would reveal, so were most of her emotions.

I tried to use conventional methods, but RAD children don't respond to normal discipline. Unbeknownst to me, these tactics are often detrimental. For a child who has spent so much time alone without things to value, and not valued herself, my punishments were inconsequential. She was relentless and I was running out of disciplinary techniques. We tried soap and hot sauce for lying. Totally ineffective. Spanking, yelling, yanking, pulling hair were all, I am ashamed to say, my early reactions to her. She seemed to know just what to do to elicit them. I would grab or pinch her when I could anticipate that she was about to act out, which was often. This was scary for a number of reasons: I didn't like to do it; I felt out of control; this wasn't how I saw myself as a parent; and Victoria didn't do anything to discourage me. She sought any attention, even negative attention, over a lonely time-out. Many of my reactions were acts of desperation and I realized this, but I didn't know what else to do. Although I felt miserable after one of these scenes, Victoria never expressed any remorse—she just parroted memorized apologies.

I would then feel terrible about how strict we were being with her. I convinced myself that Victoria needed more love. It was a very scary, destructive, and emotionally draining cycle, and she craved it. I didn't understand at the time that all my daughter was looking for was attention and I was providing an endless supply. After riding a rollercoaster of intense discipline and then more love back to intense discipline, Victoria and I kept finding ourselves in the same place. This rollercoaster was only going up and down. There was absolutely no forward motion.

Victoria knew exactly what to do to get the biggest reaction out of me. I had no idea that a four- five- or six-year-old could be so manipulative. I had no idea she reveled in the negative attention as much as the positive. I had no idea that her definition of love was attention. I had no idea that every one of my reactions was digging a deeper hole, one from which I had no means of escape.

Jay came up with the idea of Victoria running stairs or doing some other type of physical exercise for punishment. I was strongly opposed to it, at first. It seemed cruel, yet it worked. Except when it didn't. We had no back up plan. So that was never truly successful until later when we realized Jay was on the right track.

I couldn't make sense of her, my lack of compassion towards her, the guilt I felt, or the guilt others unintentionally helped me feel. Where was *our story* in all the adoption and RAD books I read? Victoria wasn't running away from home, killing the neighbor's cat, trying to burn down the house, or rejecting our physical affection which is what I read about in attachment disorder books. Where was this mother's story? I never read about the dark feelings I had or how to handle the paralyzing abuse only I, as the mother, could understand. I couldn't relate to anyone, anywhere. It was wearing me and the family down. I felt like everyone around me, who didn't live in our home, thought we were treating her so unfairly. And at times, we were.

We spent hours talking to Victoria. We tried to make her feel special and to convey our love. We wanted her to believe how wonderful it was that she was part of our family. We tried to get her to explain her actions—why and why some more. We told her exactly what she should be feeling and saying. And then she started saying the right things but her actions were the complete opposite. Her sincerity was a sword. I realized much later that she tuned us out after about the second sentence. Jay and I would both go through periods where we thought we got through to her, but we would find ourselves in the same place or two steps back the next day. Talking to RAD kids does nothing for the problem. They're bright and will give you promises that, however badly they might want to, they simply cannot keep. Victoria was just one disappointment after another and she knew it, and she really couldn't do anything about it. She didn't understand what was going on anymore than I did.

However poor her self-esteem may have been when she arrived, three years later, by the time she was seven, I can't imagine she had anything left except hatred for herself and everyone around her. We spent so much time trying to make her experience remorse for her mistakes. What we learned later is that RAD kids are never sorry enough. Never happy enough. Never full enough. Never anything enough because they are so disassociated from their feelings. Everything we did at this point and for some time after didn't make anything better. And things got a lot worse before we found any answers.

We were constantly on Victoria. It was easy to make her the scapegoat, culprit, and guilty one. She just lent herself to being the martyr. She didn't—and still only rarely— stands up for herself. She struggled to form intelligent arguments to defend herself. Because of my early reactions to her, the boys had virtually no patience for her. She didn't make it easy but I had set a precedent that she was always wrong. There came a time when she could do nothing right in my eyes and eventually gave up any attempt at trying.

I felt completely helpless. When Victoria was in trouble, didn't get her way, or felt treated unfairly—which was about all the time—she got angry. This wasn't upset; this was rage. It was big. It was uncontrolled. It was vindictive. It consumed her. She would scream, kick, break things in her room, pull her hair, and bite her lips. She would kick her walls and yell how much she hated me and how evil I was. It was terrifying to watch. I had no idea where the intensity came from because most of the time her disobedience did not justify the amount of anger. I didn't know what to do with it. I look back now and feel completely inept and ignorant, like I should have known how to redirect that anger, but I didn't. When she got mad, she became mean. It was intentional and I took it very personally. It wasn't so much the disobedience, as it was the ease and disregard Victoria had for me in these moments. I refused to be continually taken advantage of and my anger and ignorance consumed me. I couldn't even attempt to comfort her fears. I knew I was fueling them. If I couldn't figure out how to help and she had no interest in helping herself, I had nothing left to offer her.

There were moments in the mall or the grocery store when Victoria would wander off. She never seemed worried about me finding her and I eventually didn't worry if she got lost.

She didn't seem to have any fear. I stopped cautioning her if she was swinging too high, running too fast, climbing too high, or crossing the street without looking both ways.

No physical pain seemed to hurt Victoria. There were a few times when I would lash out at her, spanking and slapping her in a rage. In these moments I had to exert a tremendous restraint not to inflict serious physical harm to her. And while I certainly don't believe I was capable of killing her, I didn't think I would feel any remorse if she died.

I spent Victoria's first year at home loving her in all the ways I thought she needed. She craved my attention but wasn't interested in accepting my love. I eventually, during her second year home, gave her all my hate. I hated nearly everything about her: the way she ate, the way she smelled, and her voice when she talked. I didn't even know these feelings existed in me. Who am I? What was happening to me? I had always been able to control my feelings. I wasn't overly sensitive, but I did think of myself as understanding and caring. Now I only thought of myself as bad. I was relieved Victoria was disconnected from her feelings; it actually made it easier for me not to care. I wasn't just a bad mother I concluded, I was a bad person.

It began to frustrate me to see her appear so happy with other people. Sunday school teachers, grandparents, neighbors. It was all a façade. I began to resent people holding her, offering her treats, drinks, anything. It was the life I was trying to have with her and she was taking advantage of their ignorance. She preferred them to me. It hurt that others could provide so easily that which I as the mother was now struggling to give and had given so freely. But trying to convince people to withhold these things from a sweet, little five-year-old was met with so much misunderstanding. The average person, who hasn't experienced it firsthand, would find it nearly impossible to understand the motivations and tactics of a child with an attachment disorder. I had definitely had the experience, but I didn't have the answers to justify my intuition.

## CHAPTER 3

# *Feeling Numb to Feel Safe*

*Things don't ever seem to be going in the direction that I think they will. I don't even have a lot of expectations beyond tomorrow because my tomorrows seem to be going to places I didn't even know existed.*

If trying to figure out Victoria's behavior was an impossibility for me, I couldn't even attempt to make sense of her emotions. It wasn't just her ability to love that was underdeveloped. It was most of her emotions. She had a hard time understanding what feeling happy was like. She had no capacity of remorse. I'm not even sure what she understood about sorrow. But I know my daughter could experience anger.

The only true and consistent emotion that I ever saw in Victoria was the one she showed the most: anger. I knew she was angry. I also knew that it stemmed from fear, but I didn't know how to calm those fears. I had tried the best ways I knew how during her first year with us, but by now, two and a half years later, our inconsistency fueled her fear.

I thought Victoria's biggest fear was abandonment. I spent hours trying to reassure her that she was here to stay, because for everything I *didn't* know, the one thing I *did* know was she belonged in our family. Victoria would respond to me like she believed me, but her actions never reflected trust.

She looked so happy to everyone around her but at home she was miserable. In the first couple of years, I never heard a genuine laugh from her. She wasn't ticklish. Her smile was deceptive. Victoria would smile at inappropriate times, especially when she got into trouble and had pushed me to anger, or saw someone get hurt. She would smile no matter what she felt. I often knew what she *should* be feeling but nothing she did or said ever indicated her true emotions. She liked to tell me she had her nice smile and mean smile. The mean smile I saw often. It was coy and insincere and covered her face with empty eyes. I saw it when I would try to reason sensitively with her, when she slammed her door open putting the handle through the wall, or when she would throw things at me. She would smile when I would talk to her about feeling sad.

Those were the days that turned into years when I felt completely crazy and lonely. I couldn't make sense of her and it was literally killing my spirit. I was doing everything so carefully and yet I couldn't seem to do anything right. Victoria's face never matched her words and her words never matched her actions, and because of this, even later when I grew to understand her, I couldn't contain my hurt. I struggled at times to see beyond her face. Beyond the actions. Beyond her words. And still I was required to love her. This agony knew no words.

At first, Victoria's tolerance for pain was surprising to us. In her first week at home she went out the back door and stumbled down two stairs, landing face first. She stood up with a huge scratch on her face. No tears. No reaction. I wish I would have understood the significance of this because it was early evidence of Victoria's inability to feel. If she had a cut that started bleeding the only reaction she had was to blow on the cut. It made me think she had never been comforted when she was hurt. She didn't have anyone telling her it was going to be okay. All she had was herself blowing on the cuts trying to comfort herself.

I knew she didn't feel bad. She had no remorse. She only did what felt good to her and didn't care what anyone else thought or felt. Victoria was clearly selfish and controlling. I remember getting so angry at the ease with which she could be hateful in her outright disobedience and manipulating with her good intentions. When I would brush her teeth or comb her hair she would yell "Ow! Ow!" even though I was being gentle. I would eventually comb her hair with no regard for how it made her feel.

If she wanted it to hurt, I'd do it. I would then feel guilt for being so reactionary and I'd go talk to her on her bed. I would sit there, holding her, telling her how she was hurting me, at times with tears streaming down my face. Victoria would apologize and appear so sincere as she listened to me, but she didn't even have the capacity to feel beyond herself. I knew there were times when in her heart she truly wanted to. I just didn't know her mind couldn't allow it.

There were only three times during the first three years Victoria really opened up and I saw true emotion. The only way I could get there required really long conversations—usually in the middle of the night when her defenses were weak. I recall one night we were sitting on the stairs; she had just wet her bed. She was telling me all the ways she was sneaking drinks. I wanted to be angry. I was tired of being angry.

I was desperate to understand Victoria. The conversation drifted to the orphanage and she told me about a little boy who would always push her off her bed while she was sleeping. It hurt but she couldn't tell anyone. Tears formed in her eyes. It was the only time I can remember her being sad. It was one of the few times in two years that when I hugged her, I felt it. When I told her I loved her, I meant it.

Other times it wasn't like that. I would talk to her, usually about the orphanage, hit her to the core and she would reveal true emotion. Mostly sad, mostly hurt. But back then I didn't know how to respond to her. Instead of responding to Victoria with an increased amount of love, because she didn't seem to be accepting my love, I was just glad she was feeling something. Anything. I wanted her to languish in it. Feel uncomfortable. Want something more. She did want something more: me. But the me she was beginning to get was conditional and eventually, mean. Hateful. Vengeful.

My anger was nearly as strong as Victoria's. My fear of what was happening to me and my hurt were nearly as big as hers. I went from intense and purposeful love to intense and purposeful hate. I was tired and conditional. I couldn't do anything right. Nothing was ever enough. She didn't value anything. She didn't care. And eventually, neither did I.

I didn't want to give Victoria anything because she didn't appreciate it. I began to feel that she didn't deserve it. I began to withhold the best of everything from her. If it didn't matter to her, then I certainly wasn't going to make it matter to me. Soon there wasn't any real affection or real contempt for her. There wasn't really anything. I had nothing left to offer. We were just existing, leading parallel lives.

Certainly Victoria's brothers could see we were treating her much differently and they could also see that she was so different. But I didn't have any answers to explain what was happening to me or why Victoria acted the way she did. I knew I had to find someone who had those answers for me. For over a year I had tried to understand Victoria and my reactions to her. Nothing was making any sense. She appeared happy. She appeared affectionate. She was friendly. But it all felt empty. All I had were my feelings to validate my thoughts and they were not easily transferred into words.

At this point, Victoria was sneaking water. She was "accidentally" breaking things. She was constantly lying and peeing in her pants. She was rocking. What part of this sounds so devastating? I remember now during our third post-adoption visit, speaking in very broad terms to our social worker about how she wasn't compliant and lied often. I don't think I was specific enough. When it came to discussing Victoria's behaviors I had a tendency to downplay them. I felt responsible in some way for her actions. I didn't know how to convey my torment, and it didn't sound so bad unless you were living it. The social worker didn't seem too concerned and offered us no insight or direction. His emphasis seemed to be on Victoria's general physical health and learning.

I then talked to our pediatrician. He referred me to a prominent child psychologist in our area who had a six-month waiting list. I didn't have six months. I really didn't have six hours. The psychologist's office gave me a referral to a children's mental health facility. The doctor there was no longer practicing but arranged an appointment with one of their licensed social workers. I was so apprehensive. I believed that my reactions were the problem in my relationship with my daughter but I couldn't help but think she was also contributing to the situation.

I met with our social worker four times. During those visits I would discuss Victoria's behavior while Victoria played with toys in the waiting room. When it was time for Victoria to come in to talk with the social worker she was greeted with treats. Nothing seemed right. I took Jay to the last session and he said he wouldn't go back because he felt he was there for therapy. I knew I was in trouble when the social worker kept telling me, "You just have to remember where she's come from." How could I forget? Victoria acted like she still lived in the orphanage and we treated her like she did. I needed answers to my reactions and tools to deal with my child. During our last visit, the social worker pulled a book off the shelf, thumbed through it and threw ideas at us. Finally she gave us the name of a website at the back of the book. To say I felt discouraged was an understatement.

We were closing in on our second year with Victoria, and my heart was constructing giant barriers. I was operating on autopilot with her. I didn't know what a bad place I was in until I was able to look back at it.

We received one more referral—a child psychologist who labeled Victoria as controlling. Duh. He tried to instill fear into Victoria by telling her if she didn't start being obedient, she'd have to get shots. Oh brilliant! This girl was already operating on fear; let's give her some more to deal with. And then he recommended love and logic parenting classes for us. I was initially offended but soon realized how it could help me with some of her controlling behaviors. Unfortunately, at the same time we were planning to leave the country and live in Ireland for a year.

So we clearly had a child who operated on selfishness and manipulation, with no conscience or cause-and-effect thinking, but at the time it wasn't that specific to me. I didn't understand the extent of the damage she had endured, the trauma that prevailed, or how she could be so calculating. She was so hyper-vigilant. Victoria always knew what was going on around her, how to get the most attention and how to maintain control. She was in self-preservation mode; the only mode she has ever known. I'd later learn that Nancy Thomas, a therapeutic parent and expert on attachment disorders, identifies five ways RAD children test adults to see if they can feel safe. If they can control any of these areas, they will not feel safe.

1. They see if they can interrupt you.
2. They try to get you to repeat what you have said.
3. They try to get you to believe their lies.
4. They see if you they can steal from you.
5. They are cruel to animals.

During Victoria's first two years, we fed into all of her fears. We didn't make any huge strides in helping her, but we did have enough things working that we could at least deal with her day by day. They were just coping mechanisms that we'd acquired through trial and error. I knew what we were doing wasn't going to help Victoria get any better, it was just allowing us (me) to function at some level other than crazy. I knew that to keep her in check, I couldn't allow her to make any decisions (I'll explain why later, but most of this was lost on me then). This just stood to reason. Victoria spent her most impressionable years in an orphanage where she was told what to do every single moment of the day. She had no opportunities to make choices, experience consequences, or learn from her mistakes in a healthy environment. She came into our home and was suddenly free to decide everything for herself. It is overwhelming and mentally exhausting for RAD children to feel like they need to be in charge of themselves, and everything around them, especially at four years old. This was in addition to all the other things she had to deal with in her new life in America.

It was best if Victoria didn't play with other children. She was usually vindictive and controlling so after a while I didn't put her or the other children in that position anymore. She didn't want to share. She was demanding, bossy, and mean. And kids anywhere could pick up on this in minutes. Adults? Totally clueless because Victoria's compliance and charm was so unsuspecting to them.

I could never leave Victoria alone. I dealt with her best when she was in the same room with me doing absolutely nothing. She could not/would not entertain herself.

I knew these limits weren't doing my daughter any good but it helped me maintain my sanity and most importantly, she had no control over me. As time went on, my coping mechanisms became similar to hers. I treated her with indifference. We pushed each other away. This saved me from hurt, heartache, and disappointment. But, living with these feelings for so long made it very difficult for me to come back to a place where I could show her any type of affection.

While in Ireland and during Victoria's third year at home, things began to manifest that gave support to my feelings. I knew she was intimidated by me and didn't fully trust me. Why would she? Yet, one night as I talked to her, I brought out a purple elephant and began to talk to it. I pretended the elephant was Victoria and she answered for it. Things finally began to make some sense when she told me how often she thought about destroying her room, ripping up my clothes, and breaking everything. She told me she hated everyone in the family. I was so relieved. You must understand why: I had felt this from her but nothing she said ever indicated it. I had no idea these thoughts and others were even possible in a tiny child. I also knew our thoughts became our actions so it was no surprise that her destructive behaviors were predicated upon a very destructive mental process. But I still didn't have the knowledge of how this was all related to attachment disorders. I still believed she had a choice and she always made the wrong one. Intentionally.

This is one of the controversies surrounding attachment disorder—how much of their thought processing is a *can't* or a *won't*? I can look back and see in our first years together that Victoria's brain really wouldn't allow her to make the right choice. The only choice she had was the one that left her feeling in control, which was usually the most damaging one. It wasn't until later, when I began to build a foundation of trust with Victoria that new pathways in her brain were created that allowed her to make decisions safely.

Another instance that validated my feelings happened while we were visiting friends. Victoria came up to me on the couch and was being very affectionate. This was unusual at this point. When we got into the car to leave, I asked what that was all about. She replied, "I wanted them to think I was nice to you." Her attempts at affection were staged and ill timed. Although she knew how to appear affectionate, she didn't know how to be affectionate.

The following are insights from Breanna who was our nanny during our time in Ireland:

*When I first got to Dublin and we were living in the hotel, I remember being surprised that Jay and Jodi sent Noah down to sleep with me. This set the precedence. While I imagined spending most of my time with the little girl, I realized that she had a different set of rules to live by. In the beginning I thought it was unfortunate that she lived by such strict regulations. It seemed the boys could be wild and run about as they pleased with Tori in the background punished for previous behavior. It shocked me at the difference in treatment she received, but I had not been present for her disobedience, which is usually what got her in trouble. And after a few short days I was able to detect a subtle difference in her behavior compared to her brothers. She appeared to me a needy and spiteful little girl. What was not clear was the reason for such. I couldn't decide if it was her nature or her response to her environment. It was unusual to watch parents treat their boys in a naturally loving manner and deal with them with large amounts of patience. On the other hand I saw how easily exasperated they became with Tori. How one misstep at the beginning of the day rippled through to the night, and though they al-*

*lowed her small freedoms throughout the day, it was for short periods
as she generally misbehaved immediately.*

*I soon viewed the parent/child exchange as a struggle for power.
Victoria desperately wanting to control the aspects of her life, but being smart enough to see her day structured for her eliminating that
option. The constant need of food and water reminded me of someone with an eating disorder, which again I have always related to
control. I thought she felt unsure of her place in the world, of her
value as a person and tried to compensate. I also believed she was
completely unaware of this so a more fitting assumption I made was
that food and water were a sort of comfort for her, the one thing she
could depend on.*

*I remember watching her behaviors as she acted out, whether it
was jumping on her bed when she was sent to her room, sneaking
food, or carelessly leaving her toys outside.*

*She made friends fast on the playground and would jump in with
other little girls soon instructing them which structure they should
play on next. She had no fear of strangers and desperately wanted
friends. Though she knew how to approach them she couldn't seem to
make those lasting connections that develop into friendships.*

*Other things I remember:*

*—She took the time to color in every little geometric shape to fill in
the paper, because she saw Noah do it.*

*—Throwing the glass against the wall, leaving her bike out in the
driveway, but not really caring if it was hit and still wanting to
keep it.*

*—Smiling with vacant eyes. Lack of emotion, never a true connec-
tion with her.*

*—Feeling animosity, seeing a glimmer of satisfaction when I'd be
upset with her and make her run stairs.*

*—Teaching her to do push-ups a source of frustration for me and a
victory for her.*

*—Taking her swimming, which she really seemed to enjoy, but she didn't know how to enjoy.*

*—She was almost obnoxious as she tried to compete for attention. Needed to be reminded to let the other kids play and she could for a minute or two but it seemed to pain and upset her to watch other people having fun, being happy especially when it was a feeling she couldn't grasp while doing the same activity.*

While in Dublin we were able to meet a supportive source at an international adoption conference. Carolyn Archer is an adoptive parent and works as a consultant to assist other adoptive parents. She has written several books on the troubling behaviors that often accompany adopted children. We met with Carolyn Archer personally for about thirty minutes and it was so refreshing to connect with someone who really understood what we were talking about. She made some suggestions, gave us a couple of her books, and offered any support by telephone or other means. It was encouraging. In her books she gives specific responses to RAD kids. But what she was suggesting felt comparable to performing my own open heart surgery.

Everything was bypassing my heart at this point. I can be more specific now, but nothing was clear to me then. Victoria never developed the foundation needed to form secure attachments. That was the simple part for me to understand. The more complex part, that took time to make sense to me, was that she had no concept of love. All of the time, energy, tears, and pain I spent showing love to Victoria was processed in her mind in the exact same way "attention" from complete strangers was. My sacrifices didn't mean any more to her than the sticker she would get from the cashier at the grocery store. While in Ireland my mind couldn't make sense of this but my heart did and I was taking it all personally. It had worn me down. I had no more to offer her.

Victoria sought attention from anyone who would give it. The more the better, but even a simple smile would suffice. Nothing came freely in the orphanage or it just never came at all. She operated the same way once she joined our family. Kindness had always been conditional. Any attention directed to her, positive or negative, she thought was a result of having done something to deserve it. When someone smiled at her, or gave her something, she was convinced it was conditional. My daughter didn't even understand someone could do something nice for her just because they wanted to.

What was recommended in Carolyn Archer's book sounded completely logical to me, but my heart wanted no part of it. Essentially Archer advised going back to babyhood and reconstructing time and activities that Victoria missed out on. These included feeding the child a bottle, carrying them around in a baby sling if the child was small enough, occasionally spoon feeding them, massages, and rocking.

I started to do it. But I just couldn't. I could sense that it wasn't serving the right purpose. I felt like Victoria just could not process and make sense of my actions in a way to truly "rewire" her brain. It felt like she was sucking the life out of me. The best analogy I have is that I was pouring love into a soul full of holes and everything I did, everything I had done, just wasn't enough.

My intense acts of love in the first year and a half were more frightening to her than helpful. Victoria didn't trust me, she was protecting herself and feeling my love would have meant vulnerability. I didn't understand why she was sabotaging all of my efforts so willingly. She really wasn't; she was reacting. And eventually so was I. There was absolutely no trust on either side. Without trust, healthy bonds, including love, cannot be formed.

I spent so much time being impatient and mean to her. I never wanted to give her anything. She didn't appreciate or care about anything. She made it very difficult for me and I struggled with this. It would literally tear me up inside. I didn't know what was going on and I hated my reactions to her. This wasn't who I was. And Victoria accepted this. She didn't like it, but I think she felt she deserved it. She wanted to do better, but she couldn't and didn't understand why.

Since I didn't know what was really going on, my hurt, confusion, and numbness were all natural reactions. But the problem came when I wanted to feel justified for it all and held my child responsible. This guilt associated with my reactions to her was heavy and restricting.

For three long years—wrong or right, justified or not—I personally endured every mean look, every insincere hug, and every intentional and manipulative behavior. Victoria was on the periphery on my heart as I held onto grudges and infringements. The angst, the helplessness, the inadequacy, the elusive answers, beating myself up, left me more depleted and depressed than I understood. It was a slow, tortuous process. I thought I was the only victim, but I was the second.

CHAPTER 4

# *Learning to Respond, Not React*

---

*And while I feel so much better, Victoria seems to
have stayed the same. Now in saying that, the better
I feel comes from the control I now have. It does
not include any emotional attachment. My relationship
with her is so much better now but unless I always
want to feel like I am babysitting the neighbor's kid,
I've got to work on the bonding.*

For three years, I was manipulated and controlled by a very small girl with no conscience and total disregard for others unless it would benefit her in some way, a girl who displayed this through selfish and hateful behaviors. I couldn't make sense of the way I was feeling towards Victoria. I was, for most of the first three years she was home, helpless. I never felt hopeless because I knew someone held the answers for me, but I just couldn't find him. It wasn't until we came home from Europe in 2007, that we found an answer to hundreds of prayers—the same prayers that maintained my hope.

The first thing we did upon returning to America was find help for seven- year-old Victoria. I recall my Mom telling me about a website that dealt with RAD: Attachment.org. There I found a list of therapists in Utah and chose the closest one—fifteen miles away, in Orem. Even after all I had dealt with, I still had reservations about calling. Was there really a problem? What if it's me? Could I explain this well enough? But I also knew we couldn't go on living this way. I called Max Park, LMFT. I briefly explained my crisis and he responded by saying this was his specialty. I was cautiously hopeful. We met in his office a week later and I immediately saw that this man knew exactly what he was doing—the way he interacted with Victoria, how he could call her bluff, and confirm numerous behaviors related to attachment disorders. I was relieved. Max was able to provide me with healthy responses for Victoria. That was all I'd ever wanted—ways to respond to her. I was so tired of reacting to her in anger, looking for justification. Anger would somehow make me feel good in the moment but any satisfaction was fleeting and soon guilt would settle in. Victoria needed help (and I would soon learn, so did I). I wish I had found an attachment therapist before I brought Victoria home to help me identify the signs. One would think looking at the RAD checklist that it would be so obvious, but it wasn't about wondering if there was a problem. I clearly sensed that. I simply didn't know *what* to do.

The first and most important thing that Max required was that I, as the bonding figure and the target of most of Victoria's aggression, take care of myself. It was imperative that I make a list and do things for myself on a daily, weekly, and monthly basis. I was already sensing this need, so when Max suggested it, my list was easy to write. There are a few things that can completely take my mind off Victoria or any stress in my life. Tennis became my passion. Everyone needs to find theirs. The minute I step on the court, the game is my only focus. I think of nothing else. Running also does that for me. When I finish running, I feel strong and not just physically. Once after starting therapy I was in the same room with Victoria while I was running on the treadmill.

She looked up at me and said, "Mom, you are getting strong."

I looked at her smiling and said, "You have no idea."

The peace and understanding I receive when spending time alone in the mountains or worshipping and praying in sacred places surpasses anything else this world has to offer. It is during these times I gain real insight, direction, and wisdom. Other things include many bubble baths, pedicures, having my hair done, lunch dates, reading books, taking vacations, pulling weeds, and playing the piano. Music is powerful for me. I express a lot of emotion through songs, and my iPod is a constant companion. Journaling, prayer, and Jay were my most dependable sources of strength.

You can't help others if you are drained physically, emotionally, or spiritually. This is such a natural law, but I think, especially as mothers, we forget to live by it. It could be we don't understand the significance, do not have the support, or, sadly, feel guilty. I am so thankful for an understanding husband that recognizes and is sensitive to these needs. So while caring for myself is such a priority for me, the only challenge I find now is making sure there is a balance. I am usually out of balance spiritually. Filling my lamp takes more time and conscious effort than reading a novel or playing tennis. I've also learned to feel okay about leaving the laundry undone or piles of dishes in the sink. This allows me to go and do what gives me the energy to do everything else that is required of me. The understanding reflected in the next few pages took a very long time to acquire. It was through a lot of experiences, awareness, and Max's insight that allows me to be specific.

Because Victoria lived her first four years in three different orphanages with multiple caregivers, she did not learn how to develop healthy attachments to people. She didn't experience the consistency of having her needs met. She could not trust others around her to take care of her. She did not receive the unconditional love and security that as parents we provide so naturally. We don't think about our baby's brain development when we are holding them close, stroking their cheek, gazing into their eyes, responding to their cries, or constantly smiling at them. These are natural responses that help babies develop trust, love, and security. These seemingly insignificant actions are critical in the first three years of life. Without this foundation, children create their own survival techniques to feel safe. They begin to see that they cannot depend on or trust others around them to meet their needs. They must protect themselves. The love in their lives is either nonexistent or inconsistent. To survive with any amount of security they become very selfish and demanding. They learn to only trust themselves and refuse to relinquish control. They learn that love hurts.

Their brains are actually rewired to only rely on these survival mechanisms. It no longer becomes a conscious choice between what is right and wrong. There is no conscience. It is survival.

After reading about the circle of life in the book, *Attachment, Trauma, and Healing* by Terry M. Levy and Michael Orlans, I was able to help explain this better to Victoria. I related to her that we all have a circle of life and nobody's circle is perfect. I explained that because when she needed something as a baby, such as help, touch, or food she would cry. If those needs would have been met immediately, she would have felt good, loved, happy, and safe. She would have developed a brain that could trust. Because the gratification of Victoria's needs was delayed or never met, she began to associate being hungry with hurt, lack of touch as sorrow, and to believe that something about her was bad and unlovable. All of these conditions instilled fear. Victoria had to find ways within her power as a small helpless child to feel safe. Unfortunately RAD children find safety in being mean, physically aggressive, lying, stealing, and being sneaky and destructive. I often ask Victoria if she is using her trusting brain or her fear brain. Because she has allowed herself to begin to trust me, she can easily tell the difference.

Victoria's need to feel in control was so ingrained in who she was. It was the basis for all of her decisions. For so long, it had to be, because her most basic needs weren't being met any other way. This thought process also prohibited her from thinking rationally. Our logic, reasoning, and emotions are associated with the front of our brains. Our fight, flight, or freeze instinct (survival mode) is associated with the back of our brains. Victoria spends most of her time in the back part of her brain being fearful. That is why I used to wonder, "How can she appear to be so smart but act so stupid?" This is exactly why: She doesn't shift to the front part of her brain that allows her to reason and process. This is also why my hours of talking to Victoria would never do any good until she was free of fear and anger and able to move to the front part of her brain and comprehend what I was saying to her. All of her time in the orphanage was spent being in control trying to fulfill her needs of food, water, breathing, sleeping, and using the restroom for safety and survival. Now she has enough food and water. She has her own room and bathroom. Yet she still won't allow herself to feel comfortable with what is provided for her. You can't always see it. I've learned to be able to sense it. Because Victoria feels so out of control internally, she tries to maintain some sense of control outside of her. It expresses itself in her anxiety, tension, and a mind that is always active, evaluating what is going on around her. As long as she is stuck in the back part of her brain not trusting these basic needs to be met, the fear doesn't allow her to even begin to move on to feeling safe or loved. Her security and affection are volatile. They have to be, because there isn't a strong or confident foundation. Victoria's fear is not based on a real threat. Her fear is not protecting her and it's not allowing her to change. I often tell Victoria it's okay to be stuck, but it isn't good for her to stay stuck. I let her know she can stay there as long as she wants and I will be ready to help her when she wants to begin trying.

As Victoria tries and works towards trusting that her survival needs are going to be met, she will begin to feel security. She does, at times, allow herself to be at my mercy, safely. But only a handful of times and in those moments we make progress in her other needs of self-esteem and love. In the beginning our windows of opportunity were rare and brief.

How could I break down this wall to find these opportunities? In the beginning, and actually for a while, I didn't realize this journey would entail so much trial and error; a cycle of progress and regression constantly repeated with the days of trusting eventually getting longer and the weeks of control and defiance getting shorter. Because each child's maladaptive behaviors and each parent's capacity to deal with them are so different, so are the therapeutic approaches.

While the techniques for each child differ, what is similar, is that to build trust RAD children need consistent structure, tight boundaries, and a loving, single bonding figure, usually the mother. I am not a qualified attachment therapist, I don't hold a degree in any type of psychology, but

I found the following techniques Max suggested useful in living with and responding to a RAD child.

**No Talking in the Car.** The first rule Max suggested and we implemented was that Victoria couldn't talk in the car and if she needed to say something she could raise her hand. I would ask her what she wanted or I would tell her, "Not right now." This was brilliant. It relieved an enormous amount of stress for me because she would often use the car to attack me or her brothers verbally (and sometimes physically). If she did talk, she put one hand over her mouth (a mouth hug). If she persisted she put her head in her lap. There was a long period of months when Victoria got into the car I immediately had her put her head down because she was either touching her brothers or giving them menacing stares. This was also a good indicator to me of where she was in regulating herself. If she kept her head down, I knew it was a reflection of her self-control and obedience. But in the times she wouldn't do it, was fidgety or intentionally making noise, I knew she would be pushing me and I could expect blatant disobedience.

**Play Mat.** Another technique was to provide Victoria with a mat that became her playground. She had three activities she could do: Legos, read a book, or color. This was a *lifesaver.* This freed me from having to entertain her, or wonder where she was or what she was doing. For her, it allowed her to focus and not have to worry about making decisions and she was reaping the benefits of being compliant. I also sensed, instantly, she felt safe knowing she had a place to go. I know she welcomed the structure because she rarely left the mat or talked which resulted in playtime being over. As she maintained compliance, I added to her playthings. She liked to work on word search puzzles, and move to the table to play with Playdoh, Lincoln Logs, or a sticker book. I chose the activity and alternated it at my discretion. If I felt she had been especially obedient, I would give her a choice between two things and eventually expand her area to a room. However, typically when I gave her a choice between two things, she would name something I didn't offer her. That indicated to me she wasn't ready to make choices.

I don't know if this process sounds logical to you, but for most guests that came into our home, it seemed cruel and unusual. Unusual? Yes. Cruel? Absolutely not. But I think, with reason, it made guests feel uncomfortable because she was being so quiet on the mat she seemed perfectly obedient.

**Bare Room.** We took all of the things out of her room so she couldn't destroy them in her fits of rage. I also took the things out of her room because she felt entitled. As she began to show appreciation and self-control, we slowly added things back into her room. We put an alarm on her door so she couldn't sneak out to steal, or bother her brothers and to keep her and the family safe.

**Physical Affection.** She was only allowed to receive physical affection and treats from Jay and me until an attachment was formed. Understandably, this was very difficult for grandparents and teachers, but as long as others are undermining the parents, even with good intentions, the child will not heal.

**Consistency.** As I implemented these rules, I could immediately sense and see the benefits. But again, from the outside it was met with so much uncertainty. We looked too strict, our techniques too strange, or we were socially alienating Victoria. I would allow the pressure from others to make me question my methods and feel the need to "lighten up" on her. But for children who want to retain complete control in every situation, there isn't any room for lightening up until they begin to allow the adult to be in charge.

**No Asking.** Victoria cannot ask for anything. I still decide what she will eat and how much. I get her up in the morning and choose what she will wear. The purpose of all of this is to take away some of her control and teach her to trust me. I need her to trust that I will meet all of her needs without needing to ask me for everything. And in the past, she would ask for everything, incessantly. And if it wasn't exactly what she wanted she became angry. Eventually we want to get to a place where she can choose between two things. And then when she can, make choices on her own without specifically giving her options.

Most children, not just those struggling with attachment challenges, exhibit some of these behaviors. All children want to feel some amount of control and will push boundaries to find the safety in the structure. We do a disservice when we aren't consistent. Consistency provides a comfort and security in children's lives, even though they will at times, scream, yell, and throw tantrums. It is exhausting. It is hard work. This was magnified with Victoria. However, as children become compliant and trusting, the intense demands begin to subside. The exhaustion of providing the structure doesn't even come close to the fatigue of a child challenging you to see what they can get away with. Children aren't going to ask for rules, guidelines, and consequences, but they yearn for them. Victoria wasn't a typical child where you just did your best with good intentions. She required more. She would take my good intentions and hogtie me. I felt powerless. She required a response with consistency. This helped regulate her so she knew what to expect. And I didn't give her any second chances. There was never, "Victoria, if you do that again…"or "Remember what I said, Victoria…" She knew. She didn't forget. There needed to be a level of consistency she could depend on to build trust she had never experienced. It needed to be met before she could feel safe expressing other feelings.

Victoria usually acted out with such simple disobedience and if it wasn't damaging to others, I wanted to overlook it to avoid the rage. I did see a few things wrong with my logic. It fueled the gambler in her to keep pushing me to see what she could get away with, because it was worth it when nothing happened. It strengthened her control, which really made her sicker. She was always weighing her options. Me being inconsistent did nothing to comfort her. The pettiness of her actions at times didn't seem to warrant me living through her tantrums; however, I really didn't want to wait until the blatant, horrible, wrong choices justified the rage. That was what I was trying to avoid. I felt hopeful she would be better by the time she was a teenager. Was I setting myself up for disappointment? Did I really have any foundation to make that assumption? My mind said it was in for as long as it took, but my heart was counting on soon.

Many parents of non-RAD children I have spoken to have pieces of Victoria in their children. I sense the frustration in their voices when they talk about children's lies, their lack of empathy or being destructive. I used to find myself getting defensive in the early days when others would generalize me. I know now they could never comprehend the demands I was under but I can comprehend the helplessness they feel. I now appreciate the understanding I can offer.

There were other things that were required of her but these are the ones that I felt in the beginning were most important. Then the question became, what to do if Victoria chose not to obey? Consequences are huge in disciplining children, I tried to use natural consequences when it was possible. For instance, if it is cold outside and Victoria chooses not to wear a coat, I won't make her. And she suffers the natural consequence of being cold.

When Victoria was being defiant she wanted to push me to anger. And for many years she did. When I was finally able to understand the motivations of her actions, I tried not to engage her. There were many times I simply had to ignore it if she wasn't doing something destructive or harmful. We also learned about physical exercise and saw how Jay was on the right track with his stair climbing ideas.

What was suggested in therapy by Max for RAD children was when they don't obey to first give them a physical exercise. This can be for any disobedience every single time. Jumping jacks, running around the outside of the house, sit-ups, etc. This immediate exercise tries to break the reactionary state their brains automatically go to and also gives them an immediate consequence. This is especially important for children who haven't developed cause-and-effect thinking. If they don't do the exercise, they have to do a chore. For me, I liked a repetitive, mindless chore that didn't require constant supervision (if possible). If I knew Victoria was going to be oppositional, I liked it to be outside and she could take as long as she wanted. We used pulling weeds, shoveling, moving a rock pile, sweeping out the garage, and cleaning windows among others. If she chose not to do the chore, she would sit in her room and nothing would happen in her life until she decided to do the chore. When the chore was finished, she then had to go back and also complete the physical exercise. Victoria never really got to the room stage because I always had her do a chore she could finish in her own time. She could finish in fifteen minutes when she was compliant but she has been known to take five hours or more. When Victoria had accomplished whatever was required of her, her thought process had usually moved to the more logical part of her brain. We could then reason with her. We could ask her what happened and what she could do to make it better. We were teaching her more than just cause-and-effect thinking. She was learn about accountability, restitution, and empathy. And we were able to be positive with her for completing the exercise or the chore.

It was interesting when we started this because it took away so much control, and that was frightening to Victoria. Again, the way most RAD children manifest fear is through anger. I would call her on everything she did no matter how insignificant it was—for example, if she was hitting her brother, eating with her mouth open, glaring at others, being disrespectful, taking too long to finish a task, or trying to direct me. Initially she wouldn't even attempt the exercise. I would tell her to give me twenty jumping jacks and if she replied with "What?" or "Why?" I immediately shifted to a chore. But mostly she would just begin screaming about how mean I was and how much she hated me. I can remember days (and there still are occasional ones) where she would yell a blood curdling scream that seemed to go on forever. If pulling the weeds, she would sit in the dirt, cover herself with it, and pee on herself staying there for hours. Some days she would pull on her clothes, her skin, and her hair in such a rage. She hated that she had absolutely no control over me. She was at my mercy and she was terrified. But she would eventually finish. These scenarios would play out daily for about three months leaving me stuck at home, with no signs of reprieve.

It was so exhausting trying to be consistent and outlast the rage. Also trying to ignore all the negative behavior that was clamoring for attention

*There are things that feel good to Victoria that shouldn't: lying, being sneaky, and manipulating. Her need to feel good is met best by attention. Any kind. If she doesn't get it freely, she will demand it negatively. She wants to get caught in her lies, stealing, and annoying behaviors. It makes it hard to know when and how to respond so I am not feeding into the destructive cycle, because I also need to exercise some consistency in giving consequences for disobedience. I can't let her see my frustration, impatience, or helplessness. It feeds her destructive cycle and helps her feel in control when it looks like I'm not.*

was equally exhausting. This was demanding, but when Victoria realized that this was going to happen every single time, she began to choose her battles—usually to test me. The fits of rage began to decrease.

She got to a point where she didn't do nearly as many chores but her occasional disobediences that demanded a consequence resulted in sending her outside to move a rock pile. She would stand outside, look around at the neighbors' windows on both sides, scream at the top of her lungs, and demand attention. She would stop, look around some more for any warm bodies to notice her, and continue her scream fest. Until I explained our situation to the neighbors, I thought for sure the police were going to show up at my door.

When I spoke to the neighbors they were very concerned. This was a difficult situation to understand. Most people, even though they can't really comprehend the complexities of the disorder, comprehend it at some level. Others simply don't get it.

If Victoria was breaking rules in the grocery store by touching everything and not staying right by me, or if we were in the car and she was kicking the seat and licking her fingers and smearing the windows, I wouldn't say anything to her. Most behaviors I had to ignore until we got home. Then I would simply tell her she had to clean all the windows in my car and wipe down all of my seats. While it took a lot of patience to ignore deliberate negative behaviors, it didn't do me any good to feed into them at the grocery store or threaten her with a chore. If I told her she would be doing a chore when she got home, she would self-destruct. It only encouraged her to act out more as her mind told her she had lost that battle.

The discipline that worked best for Victoria was a delayed consequence, but I had to be ready for retaliation. A delayed consequence came when she least expected it and it was totally out of her control. For instance, if she is totally disobedient and passive-aggressive during church—standing up, pulling her dress up, talking loud, and yelling my name—my anxiety level skyrockets. She then sits down and begins to rub my arm and hands.

I feel the insincerity and it is making me sick that she is touching me. I don't respond or react. Then, the next week, when it is the children's program, I tell her she cannot participate because I don't trust she will be reverent. It is hard. There are so many times I just want to let it all go.

While at the park, if Victoria wouldn't stay where I told her to play, I would require her to have a time-out next to me. This required her to sit next to me in a perfectly still position, back erect so she could breath deeply and reach a place where we could talk about what happened. She would stay there. Never trying to get up. Never asking to leave. But instead she would start in on all her passive-aggressive tactics to get a reaction out of me. And any reaction would suffice. She would begin to pick grass and pretend to toss it up but intentionally throw it on me. She would start to kick my chair softly. She would stare at me. Start pulling on her hair. Chewing on her shirt. Anything to get me to react and give her attention. It would take every patient part of me to ignore the incessant behaviors. One right after another. All Victoria wanted was for me to say, "Stop that!" Even a mean glare would satisfy, for the moment. And at times I just wanted to do it so that it would all be over with, but it only encouraged the destructive cycle. She fed off negative attention so I would simply say things like, "Oh it looks like you aren't strong enough to go play on the swings," or "Thanks for letting me know you can't handle being around others right now." I would wait until the next day when we were at the park again and instead of letting her swing I would say, "No, I can't trust you to swing with the way you acted towards me yesterday." I would understand the rage because I was in total control.

When Victoria would color she would always break her crayons. So I would only give her three crayons. If I walked back into the room, seeing them in pieces I would simply say, "Wow, that is so cool, now you have six crayons instead of three." I can still see the irritation in her eyes when she didn't get the desired reaction from me. Eventually breaking crayons lost its effectiveness. Many of her behaviors required this method of acceptance. Victoria needed to know that I accepted her the way she was and that I could handle whatever she did. If she didn't experience this is me, she could never ever trust me.

I remember early in therapy, Max had us make a trust chart on Victoria's wall. It had about twenty marks and about every fifth one had a privilege attached to it. As she did well during the day, we would move up the marks until she earned a privilege. I loved this idea. It was tangible for her to see we weren't the bad guys. She was the one in charge of her choices. But it failed miserably for her. She would work hard until she just about got to the privilege and would purposely ruin it. She especially liked to sabotage the good in her life because she really didn't believe she deserves it. For example, if I know that she will be invited to a birthday party, I don't tell her we are going until we are about ten minutes from the party. In those ten minutes she will do everything she can think of to ruin her chances of going—kick the seat in front of her, unbuckle her seatbelt, hit her brother, or makes annoying noises. It is sometimes difficult to know when she is ruining privileges she doesn't think she deserves and trying to push us away, as opposed to trying to exert control over a situation.

The most difficult thing for me was ignoring her. She would steal food and hide the wrappers in the same place every time: under her sink. Now, I don't even confront her about it. If she ever wants to talk to me about it I simply say, "Victoria when you steal food it just shows me you aren't ready to trust yet and receive privileges." When Victoria had muscle eye surgery to correct a lazy eye the doctor recommended Victoria wear regular reading glasses to help with nearsightedness. I knew this was going to be a disaster. She proceeded to take the screws out of both sides and eventually broke them in half. We, with no fanfare, dutifully mended them with duct tape. She soon ruined them beyond repair, and purposefully lost the next pair. I promised I wouldn't buy her another. At her next appointment the doctor asked Jay if she had been wearing her glasses.

"No," he replied, "She breaks or loses them."

"They aren't expensive," the doctor responded. "You will have wasted your money on the surgery if you don't make her wear them."

"It isn't about the money," said Jay. "She intentionally does these things."

"Well, can't you just send her to her room?" came the doctor's pathetic reply.

Jay insisted we buy her one more pair. I made the mistake of buying them for her while she was with me. I felt her control one day as I ran into my cousin, Camie, who noticed Victoria's glasses.

"Those are cute glasses," Camie said.

"My mom bought these for me. She said she would never buy me another pair, but she did," replied Victoria with malicious glee.

Camie was unaware of the manipulation; I felt every bit of it. And ignored it.

As I said earlier Victoria would pee in her bed, on her floor, anywhere she wanted to exert some control. My early reactions were disastrous. She fully engaged me but I learned that was another behavior I had to approach with indifference. After I started working with Max, Victoria was required to take all her bedding to the laundry room and scrub out her clothes in a bucket. She spent many hours cleaning the floor and her carpet. To build trust my mind worked as hard as hers to anticipate delayed consequences, ignoring deliberate negative behavior, trying to find the sincerity in the positive, deciding what to respond to or not and stay consistent. It was hard. It was time consuming. I had to constantly be thinking one step ahead of her. It didn't allow me to be the mother I wanted to be to my other children, or truthfully, a great wife, friend, sister, or daughter. But I knew it wouldn't last forever. And when that time came, I would have already learned so many lessons, that I would be a far better mother, wife, friend, sister, and daughter than I could've ever hoped to be.

Jay and I attended therapy sessions with Victoria weekly. At the beginning of each session, Victoria would sit outside the office while we discussed her behaviors that week with Max and asked any additional questions. Max would then bring Victoria in and talk about her behaviors and emotions. Towards the end of the session he would give her homework for the next week.

There were a series of steps that we worked on with Victoria to initiate bonding. On her part it was based on the acronym Max created: AROUSES. *Affection, Respect, Obedience, Understanding and Responsibility, Service, Empathy and Sacrifice.* These are placed in order, building upon each other, until we have reached the most important—sacrifice.

Affection. I was surprised to see affection at the beginning of the list but it can be faked. Victoria clearly loves the signs of physical affection. It used to make me think that everything was going well until I eventually understood that the emotional affection was only going one way. Victoria's attempts to love were hollow. Her physical expressions had nothing to do with loving me at all. They were just motives to get me to give her more attention. And the attention I was giving her was short-lived. She took it, felt good in the moment, and let it go. That was why simply providing more love is not the answer for RAD children.

This affection would include random hugs, daily cuddle time, reading a story, or singing a song. It needed to be done consistently. As I did this, Victoria began to understand and return appropriate affection to me.

**Respect.** This required Victoria to use kind words and manners while maintaining eye contact. Max gave Victoria five rules and she had them memorized after the first time he told her, but following them took her a few years. The Rules of Therapy are:

1. Max is the boss.
2. Maintain eye contact with person you are talking to.
3. Tell the truth.
4. Share your emotions.
5. Ask for help.

I needed Max to be the boss because I certainly didn't know what I was doing. But almost as important, was by allowing him to be the boss, any rules Victoria didn't like (which were just about all of them) he could take the blame. I had to enforce them but any aggression about the rules was directed at him and I didn't have to "pay" for it.

Maintaining eye contact was very difficult for Victoria. It implied some kind of submission and she was held accountable for actually paying attention to me.

Being honest was obvious but seemed to go against everything Victoria was. I had to work hard, being diligent and consistent to get her to trust me and eventually tell me truths that she wouldn't feel safe telling anyone else.

It was difficult for Victoria to share her emotions because she either didn't display them or she didn't really know what the emotion was. I spent many days needing to tell her what emotion she was feeling or the emotion she should be feeling at that moment. I think feeling bad has been her most difficult emotion to experience. She lacked the conscience to feel remorse and her fear went straight to anger. At the end of the day, I would talk about our four basic emotions: mad, bad, sad, and glad. We would both name things we had felt that day with each of those feelings.

Asking for help was hard for Victoria because she wanted to do it her way even when she knew it would be easier with help. I had to prompt her many times before she began to be willing to seek help.

As a way to show respect she was to respond to everything I asked of her with "Yes, Mom." This also worked great with my other kids.

**Obedience.** We needed Victoria to be able to follow directions. When she did things right away, fast and snappy and right the first time, she would learn that obedience was a form of showing love to me. But as I've already written, she had no desire to follow my directions for a very long time. It took more patience than I thought I could ever possess. I had to outlast her defiance. It has all paid off now but even reflecting on it brings back my feelings of exhaustion and loneliness. My demands to get her to obey were so misunderstood by others.

**Understanding and Responsibility.** This helped Victoria realize what others were saying to her. She had to not only know what we were saying but she had to repeat it, feel, and want to follow through with what she was being told. She needed to maintain eye contact, listen, ask questions for clarification, repeat back what we wanted her to do, and validate the emotions of others. She was usually willing to do this when she was at a place where she was obeying and beginning to feel the good that comes from doing what she was told.

**Service.** We would give Victoria opportunities to do something helpful for someone else. This would help her learn that doing service makes herself and others feel good, as well. She could do this on her own, secretly, without being asked or I could guide her to find opportunities. Max suggested that Victoria and I together provide anonymous service for members of our family. It was a great suggestion that allowed her to not only feel the benefits of service, it gave us opportunities to experience rare positive moments together.

**Empathy.** This meant Victoria would have to feel beyond herself and do something about it. This is the hardest type of love for children to understand. It's even hard for adults. We had to set Victoria up for moments when she had to recognize what someone else was feeling and respond to it. For instance, we would stage Jay looking frustrated and she would need to ask him what was wrong. If he said he couldn't find his keys, she would offer to help.

**Sacrifice.** If empathy was difficult for Victoria, sacrifice went against everything she ever was. We first started with requiring her to give up something most important to her, food. She had to give up her dessert every day to a family member. For months she didn't do it willingly and occasionally we would force her to. Slowly she began to offer her treats to others. It was a miracle to witness. She doesn't do it all the time but she now thinks about it. We also point out all the sacrifices we make on her behalf so she can recognize our love, because if it isn't a tangible thing, directed right towards her, she misses it.

If I had had this knowledge in the beginning, it would have made Victoria's life and mine much easier. These were things I needed to know. When we implemented these rules, our lives changed completely. Max hears this from many mothers with RAD children. I don't understand why this information isn't more widely given or presented in a way that is more easily understood.

The first part of the therapy process focused on her behaviors. We needed to get her to a place where she was mostly compliant. No one can tell you how long this will take. I cannot say it enough: comparing RAD experiences is like comparing apples to oranges. There are some definite similarities but the differences are immeasurable. Each child's behaviors and parent's reactions are unique. Throughout this process I wanted to find myself replicating the experiences Max had with other RAD mothers. Usually I want to be anything but ordinary, but in this process I wanted everything to be predictable. It hasn't been and it wasn't meant to be.

The logical part, which was everything we initiated to turn control back over to Jay and me, happened fairly quickly. We were doing some of those things already. Victoria wasn't choosing to relinquish control; we just weren't giving her the ability to be in control. She continued to demand to be in charge but it was no longer successful. The intensity of her demands still amazes me. Even four years later, she is as vigilant as ever. It's disheartening when she stops trying to make her life better. I just want to make her but it isn't possible. I've got to give her the space she needs to work on changing her heart and accepting her for who she is.

After the first few sessions Victoria knew what was required of her. Now what would be required of me, the bonding figure? I had no idea that what was going to be required of me would stretch me beyond anything I had done in the previous three years or in my entire life for that matter.

To form trust I had to not only be consistent in expecting her to obey, but I had to provide her with unconditional affection, something she had never had in her life. Here we were at the beginning of Max's acronym and I couldn't get past the first letter. I was still reeling from the previous three years. I was still far from understanding my daughter. I was still taking all of her behaviors so personally. I didn't know how to stop. My mind wanted to make sense of why she reacted the way she did but clearly my heart was lagging behind. How was I going to do this? Max would make "simple" requests of me to show Victoria affection: random hugs, read a book at night, cuddle time, rub her back, etc. I honestly told him I couldn't do it. I was being asked to do those very same things I had done so carefully and deliberately in the beginning. The thought of doing so many similar things again had me paralyzed with fear. This was my part of the story I never read anywhere.

# CHAPTER 5

# *Stumbling Blocks*

*Most of the time Victoria is on guard. Occasionally
she offers to help, appears endearing, or writes
me a love note in church. Is this an unattached child?
In these moments, when I won't allow myself to take
them for what they are worth, I feel like the unattached
mother. To find us on the same page, at the same moment,
with the same intentions is nothing short of a miracle.*

*I* can write all day about the matter-of-fact stuff, the consequences, behaviors, and therapeutic approaches, but the intensely personal part of the
story is much harder. I am not even close to perfect and this journey just
confirmed that for me. This is my struggle. Everyone has one. Mine is personal, specific only to me in how I dealt with it. But what I want to accomplish in this book, especially for those who find themselves loving under the
most difficult of circumstances, is the comfort in knowing that someone is
dealing with similar struggles. There is not a one-size-fits-all fix for the emotional challenges RAD children present to parents, especially mothers.

There were some major stumbling blocks in my way that hindered my
helping Victoria. There were times when my heart was at war with what I
knew I should be doing and my ability to do it. I just couldn't provide the
physical affection required of me. I didn't want to sit down and read her a
book. It wasn't even the last thing I wanted to do; it was the one thing I
*never* wanted to do. Thankfully, Jay could do all the things I couldn't do
until I could do them. My heart had become so bitter and resentful. Even
with the knowledge I had after working with Max, that all her acts against
me weren't so much to hurt me but reactions of a broken and sick child, I
couldn't seem to let it go.

I can remember times when even the thought of showing Victoria some kind of physical affection was traumatic to me. I felt like I could do it, but literally, when I saw her face—you know, the one everyone falls in love with so quickly—my heart would not allow what my mind knew had to be done. I couldn't see beyond the face. I wouldn't see her heart. I knew that buried by fear was a little girl with so much good to give, but I couldn't see it. I wasn't allowing myself to. It never failed, for instance, on my worst days there would be a talk in Church on charity. I was a mess. I knew I was capable of being kind and generous. What was keeping me from doing this for Victoria? I wanted this to be fixed. I wanted to do what I needed to do for her. I sent the same email to Max and my dad asking for help. I sent the email to Max because I knew I couldn't be the first mom with this problem and I sent one to my Dad because I felt he understood what my heart was capable of.

Max responded with suggestions that had worked for other mothers. I could pretend to see a baby, or one of my other children's faces when I looked at Victoria. I could imagine her as having cancer or some other disease because she really was sick on the inside even though she looked perfectly fine on the outside. He also said there was no magic trick to solve our problems. I knew none of those suggestions were going to work for me.

My dad sent me back an email I still treasure. He reminded me of the charity I did indeed have and had since my youth. I couldn't seem to find it at that time, but his confidence in me and other precious truths in that letter were a comfort. This is an excerpt from the email.

"...I can't really know completely what you are experiencing, but I do know that you are hurting. This is what I know, that you have shown that you have a gift. It is that you have a love to help everyone. It is called charity, and I am speaking of the pure love of Christ. It is in you and has been from your youth. It will come, it is a promise from the Lord that he will bless us and lift us in our time of need.

*You are His faithful daughter and He has a plan for you and Tori.*
*Remember His answers are 'Yes, Later, and I have a better plan'."*

Things didn't change instantly. I would imagine the time involved is a distressing stumbling block for many parents trying to love children that are abusive emotionally and often physically. RAD children, and even healthy children to some extent, find the buttons to push that can trigger us to react. They study our behaviors and target those areas in which they can wear us down. A healthy child occasionally does this to get what they want. A RAD child constantly does this to survive. Trying to figure out what those buttons are and replacing those reactions with patience and love is too personal to have anyone figure out for you. It does require a deep introspection and willingness to change. I know each of us have our own ways of dealing with difficulties in our lives, and for me, it required a spiritual change.

That change was initiated by Max about three months after we had started therapy. He was in my home after meeting with Victoria's kindergarten teacher. He spoke of my bitterness and resentment. He validated my deep hurt. We talked about repentance and forgiveness. I knew he was right. If I was to expect any changes from people around me, especially Victoria, they first had to come from within me.

The range of emotions I had felt during Victoria's first three years at home were anger, rage, helplessness, torment, fear, sorrow, confusion, and so much hurt. What I still find completely astonishing is that I had reached the very same place where Victoria was. My feelings were the exact ones she had dealt with her entire life. It had taken the adult me to rise above them and forgive. I fought with myself, as I knew my love for her was so conditional. I was waiting for a sincere apology or genuine remorse for all the manipulation, deceit, stress, and anxiety—conditions I was beginning to realize she might never meet. I needed to let it go. Let it all go. I spent many hours studying scripture, pleading in prayer, and reading the *Peacegiver* by James L. Farrell. This a beautiful book about how Christ can help us heal strained relationships. I am sorry now. I never thought I would have anything to be sorry for. It was never about me and now I see, in these moments, it was all about me.

Forgive a seven-year-old? Who finds themselves needing to do this? I do. I had to. Most of Victoria's behaviors were executed without a conscience or empathy. She didn't care what she did as long as it felt good, and she paid no attention to how her actions might make others feel. Without knowing this, these behaviors I endured all day long looked purposeful, vindictive, and evil. I was visiting Victoria's kindergarten class one day when a little boy came up to me. "You are Victoria's mom, aren't you?" he said. "Yes," I replied. "She is the meanest girl in the class. She is evil." I felt this way for over three years. Every one of her actions seemed intended to hurt me. And at times, what she did was deliberate, but I also think she was so consumed with herself she couldn't even think what the consequences of her actions might be doing to me. This was another instance where my heart and mind were in an all-out battle. I finally got to a place where I could understand and forgive her for what she had done to me, but I continued to take her actions personally.

Hindsight is very clear but I assure you nothing about this process was. It was confusing, frustrating, and painful. I knew every Monday we went to therapy to find ways to help Victoria. This meant each Monday something was going to be required of me. Max could see my struggle but I know he didn't understand why everything was so hard for me. He was very sensitive when he made the gentle suggestion to explore my feelings and forgiveness towards Victoria. This was a very important and personal journey for me. She didn't need my forgiveness, but I needed to forgive her. I had to convince my heart she truly did not know what she was doing and I had to let it all go. It was such a weight and I had carried it around for so long I didn't even realize how heavy it was until I began to feel my heart mend. I was ready to let it go. But in letting it go, I had to tell myself that moving forward and leaving the resentment and bitterness behind didn't diminish what I had endured.

The initial months of therapy were about building trust so we could eventually break down Victoria's walls. I thought that freeing my heart from all the resentment would be enough to start helping Victoria heal. I was in a far better place, but I was still allowing things she did to hurt me. And I also felt an enormous amount of pressure to initiate and form trust with her so I could be the person she would bond with. I felt I needed to do everything that was required of me so I would not be guilty for her not learning to trust. It was so important she begin to prefer me and trust me.

This was a problem. Any trust we formed early in her arrival had been destroyed by our ignorance, inconsistency, and impatience. Max really didn't have anything to work with. Not only was the child damaged; the mom was depleted and the dad just trying to make sense of what this girl was doing to his wife. While Jay knew something was terribly wrong, I was so alone in this anguish. My boys, while at times irritated and confused with Victoria, continued to be protected. I had given so much to Victoria in those first few years that I began to shut down. The abuse of my trust, my love, and the guilt…there are no words to describe the burden I felt, to know how I should feel toward my daughter, when I couldn't. And it is this that is so painful: even after I learned the motivations behind her behaviors, my heart continued to lag behind.

I remember begging Max, "Just tell me what to do and I'll do it," because I felt so much pressure to do for Victoria what I didn't even feel I was capable of. I did finally feel a slight change of heart. I found it easier, but not easy, to show her consistent affection. I would touch her head, stroke her cheek, hug, or read to her a few times a day. They were baby steps but at least it was progression. I rarely told her I loved her, only when I could really mean it. She wouldn't respond, which I was thankful for, because I was tired of the days when she only said the "right" thing.

After letting go of the hostility, I could provide the affection now and it worked. For her. But I couldn't maintain it. I couldn't seem to find the strength to give her a second chance. The most painful part was in the evening. I would take her defiance all day long. I compare it to Chinese water torture where they strap you down and a drop of water lands on your forehead every few seconds. It's only water, right? But it is torment- ing. That is exactly what her seemingly insignificant controlling behav- iors felt like all day long. And then, I was supposed to go in and cuddle with her, feed her a piece of chocolate, and act unaffected by it all? The smile that greeted me screamed *conditional*. Yet, I could not be. I had to begin with a clean slate each morning, no matter what happened the day before. Nearly every day was a lesson in forgiveness. It was so hard. I needed someone to understand why it was so agonizing. I needed that someone to be Max.

But he seemed so unconcerned with me. He definitely wanted me to be in a place where I could help Victoria, but I don't think he really cared how I got there. Yet, I needed him to care because without it I would never get where Victoria required me to be. I demanded he have some sincere regard for my personal journey. He insisted he did, but he never once asked about me. He said he was thrilled with my progress, but he had no idea where I had come from. He thought I was an awesome mom, but I hadn't done anything awesome. If he knew my story he would clear- ly see that. He told me Victoria was mild but if he knew my torment he would have known that would have been better left unsaid. If he knew the anguish I felt living day to day with this child he would have never told me I should enjoy parenting a RAD child. So many things he innocently said verified that he had no idea that having me just "go through the mo- tions" would never change my true feelings towards Victoria.

I also knew I was expecting too much from Max. I realized he wasn't what I needed him to be. Whatever that was, I wasn't even sure. But I was on a rampage to demand that he be all of those things to me and when he wasn't, I was frustrated and angry. I accused him of being ignorant of my struggles. I was indignant that he couldn't understand the source of my pain without me having to tell him because I couldn't. I knew the pain I felt was more than Victoria. I was feeling childlike. I knew I was somehow making it worse than it should have been. I needed him to tell me why.

My demands overwhelmed Max. My pain and frustration were so real. I would lash out in emails because it felt safer that way, but that medium is not conducive to expressing accurate emotion. By the time my outrage traveled through the ether, it was lost on him. I knew he felt incompetent responding by email. Yet I battered him, hoping that at some point he could make sense of the madness. I just figured since he was the therapist, and had worked with hundreds of mothers, that he had dealt with others just like me. Apparently my reactions weren't in his "other mothers" files. This was what he did—dealt with people, all day long. Well and sick, normal and me—completely crazy. Understand me, Max!

We went to therapy every Monday. By Saturday, stress would kick in and I would want to cancel. I knew Max was what Victoria needed, the only way she was going to get better. So I would go, never canceling, realizing that I couldn't even manage to do what had been asked of me the week before.

The previous three years and the demands of our new therapeutic routine had left me in pieces. I had finally reached a place where I could be a bit more open-minded about Victoria and do things for her. I thought that was the root of all my turmoil. But it wasn't. What was? What had me so emotional? I was wearing my heart on my sleeve. I couldn't find the energy to do things. I was lethargic and found the least bit of responsibility was debilitating. I began to realize I could not do anything until I was whole. I couldn't pretend any longer waiting for it to become real. It wasn't working for me. It was scary for me to stop therapy. I was worried about Victoria, me, and the support, but it was worth it just to free myself of the stress that I encountered every week going into that office. So nearly six months after we started therapy, we stopped.

# CHAPTER 6

# Breaking Down My Emotional Fortress

*The therapist is a tool; his usefulness is
dependent on me, the worker.*

After ending our relationship with Max, I continued to feel weak and childlike. I felt dependent and needy. But mostly, I hurt. I didn't understand so many things when it came to Victoria. But what I did know was that it seemed more agonizing than it should have been. I knew she was challenging and aggravating, but this was anguish. She was hurting me with her insincerity, her mistrust, her intentional disobedience, her manipulation, and her lack of remorse. I knew that my reactions to her made everything more difficult than it should have been but I couldn't make sense of her or me. I was looking from the inside out. I couldn't see everything objectively. When I stopped therapy, I didn't know how I was going to fix myself. But I was beginning to realize I needed someone who could see from the outside in. This was a problem. I don't let people on the outside in. This was a part that was so intensely personal. I wanted to share it; I didn't want to share it; I wanted everyone to understand it; there is no way I could ever explain it all. I had to look to my past to make sense of my present.

I stopped therapy for Victoria and felt relief from the demands, yet the relief didn't last. Something just wouldn't leave me alone. Max was constantly on my mind, but I knew that he certainly couldn't provide me with what I needed. I hadn't thought about how I was going to fix what I couldn't even diagnose. I had finally begun to make some sense of Victoria. Now, here I was, trying to understand me. I didn't know what to do, so about two weeks after terminating therapy and with limited options, I called Max. I told him I thought I was suffering from depression. I seemed to have many of the symptoms but I didn't know what was going on. He scheduled an appointment for the following day.

What he couldn't see in me and I didn't know, is RAD children, with all their mechanisms for survival, often aggravate unresolved trauma that has occurred in the mother's life.

It is tall. It is secure. A sign hangs from it reading, "No Trespassing." I have always known it. I built every piece of this wall around my heart. My heart is cautious. It is fearful. It lacks trust and confidence. It is the only heart I have ever known. You can stand back. And watch. You think you see confidence, strength, and faith. But what you won't see, is it's standing on shaky ground.

I have managed to live my life behind this wall, trying to be what I wanted to be yet never really getting there. I didn't know the wall was holding me back; I thought it was protecting me. I even felt strong behind this wall. And then, the ground began to shake. The bricks began to fall. My heart was exposed. The cause of the quake was subjecting me to the torment I was protecting myself from: the pain of things that I had left behind so long ago—but they never left me.

I discovered this while sitting across from Max. He pulled out a legal pad and I began to reflect on my past. I was careful, trying to answer his questions and offering nothing more. I was so reluctant, knowing I would be sharing parts of me only I had known. He began sketching my history into a series of arrows, dotted lines, and circles—my attachment cycle. It looked complex, but I began to feel the weight of the world lift off my shoulders as I spoke. While scribbling away, Max shook his head and said, "This makes sense." What a relief! This meant I was making sense. This was all I ever wanted—to understand Victoria and to have Jay and Max finally understand me. I won't forget how scary it felt to open up to Max. How my heart was so constricted I could hardly breathe. How my hands turned cold and my blood stood still. I had been tormented by my past, confused by my present, and uncertain for my future.

My father was the stabilizer in our family. His humor and patience were a comfort to me. His love and affection were a security for me. When I was about ten, my nurturing father walked out and fear walked in. Fear, the destroyer of trust. He became a stranger. I lived in a world I didn't understand. I was a child and didn't know what questions to ask, I didn't know what to feel, so I just pretended it was all okay.

I was left with a volatile and reactionary parent. My mother struggled to raise six children and was angry and impatient. I tried to do the right things but, it always seemed like she was just waiting for me to be wrong. I never felt like my successes were recognized or encouraged. My best didn't ever seem good enough. I wasn't good enough. I couldn't even appreciate the things I did well.

I was intimidated by my mother. I was afraid of her because I didn't really know who she was—outside of the home she seemed completely different. Fear, the destroyer of trust. But I held it together, found strength in myself and pretended it was all okay.

Around this same time I was the victim of sexual abuse. I was small. I was confused. I felt guilt. I felt shame. I felt weak. I felt unworthy. I felt like I had no one to turn to. I thought the adults around me knew, but they didn't keep me safe. I was scared. Fear, the destroyer of trust. I kept it all inside, and pretended it was all okay.

I felt abandoned. I felt inadequate. I felt weak. I felt so very lonely. I was teased and tormented. I didn't know where to find relief. I had a sliver of hope that saved me from destructive mistakes, but it didn't stop the wall from surrounding my heart and vowing protection. I worked hard to do the right thing and appeared confident as fear pushed deeper into my heart.

When Victoria arrived, her need for control targeted my fears, and was fueled by my reactions. I was doing everything right for her but it was never enough. I had felt this inadequacy before.

All my careful efforts were not being appreciated and Victoria offered me no incentives to keep on giving. I had felt this disregard before.

*I know of the power that is in Christ, the power not only to create the worlds, and divide the seas but also to still the storms of the human heart, to right life's wrongs, to ease and eventually remove the pain of scarred and beaten souls. There is no bitterness, no anger, no fear, no jealousy, no feelings of inadequacy that cannot be healed by the Great Physician. He is the Balm of Gilead."*

—Robert Millet

She didn't seem real and her emotions were insincere. I had witnessed this frustrating confusion before.

Victoria was taking advantage of my trust. I was being manipulated. I had felt this abuse before.

I felt violated and confused. I became the very mother I vowed not to be. I was doing and feeling things I didn't think I was capable of. Guilt took up residence and confronted me on every side.

I began to see and make the connection to what it was in me that caused me to react so strongly to my daughter's behaviors. All of us have some conflict from our past that remains unresolved—some more than others. Many can live their lives despite it. It may reveal itself in different ways not causing enough torment to require facing it. Or we may not have enough strength to deal with it. Trauma can ignite it. When Victoria came into my life, she tipped over my psychological apple cart. My reactions were confusing and overwhelming. Only I could pick up the pieces.

I don't know all of the techniques therapists use to approach past trauma, but for me, Max chose the Gestalt approach of the empty chair. At the beginning of the first session I looked at Max, and asked him with all the vulnerability I had, "Please tell me this is important and significant because otherwise I don't want to do it." Max answered with no hesitation and complete humility, "Yes, it is very significant." At that moment I left my safe harbor, trusted Max, relied on his reassurance often, and completed months of therapy in a few short weeks. I had needed it to be intense and quick, and it was.

The powers of friends, family, or therapist to heal and to help you are limited. There were matters of the heart for me that required a spiritual change. I had to rely on my faith. My faith in a Heavenly Father, who is very aware of me and my circumstances, and a Savior, Jesus Christ, who through His divine love, and knowing my every heartache healed what no person could fix.

There were too many things I was hanging onto that were hardening my heart. I turned these things over to the One that had already taken them. I began to let them go—hurt, anxiety, fear, doubt, and abandonment. My capacity to feel and love increased. I realized all of these negative feelings were holding me back. Pieces of me that had been numb were now more intense. I needed to be whole if I was going to help Victoria.

It helped that my parents are happily remarried to each other. I have a better understanding of my mother that has improved our relationship. I can reflect on the past and see everything more clearly, without pain. I didn't know it was possible. I feel at peace with the past, more love in the present, and a bright hope for the future. The pieces of me fit back together. I am whole. I am more empathetic and loving. I came through this part of my journey reminded of the woman who felt weak, helpless, depleted, and unsure and reached out with just enough faith to touch the hem of the Savior's garment. And His reply to her applies timelessly to me: "Daughter, be of good comfort, thy faith hath made thee whole…"

I am certain, Victoria will deal with more heartache and sadness than most adults will in their lifetimes. I encountered her sorrow, every single day for four years. She doesn't manifest it in childlike grief. She manifests it in anger. In my ignorance, and in fighting with my own demons, I could not calm her fears; and worse, I couldn't even begin to heal her wounds.

In my fight to protect myself from what I thought were her evil and malicious behaviors, I know I instilled more fear because I felt so out of control. She picked up on the fact that I didn't know what was going on. She didn't either, but she was aware enough to figure out that based on my reactions, nothing was going to get better anytime soon. She continued to act like she still lived in the orphanage and she had turned us into orphanage workers. I simply didn't know how else to act with her. All of our reactions, while appearing scary and vengeful to us, were commonplace for her. We had to show her a different way. A better way and convince her of it. It was a bit more challenging to do three damaging years later, but it was still possible.

I also knew that in my worst moments of weakness, with a heart at war, I just inflicted more pain and hurt into a little girl's soul that was already in pieces. It is true, I simply did not know. But I was also weak. That is a truth that whispers from the corners of my mind. There is no justifying it, there is no one else to blame, there are no good excuses.

So much of the pain Victoria has borne, I had endured during my childhood. I could not make sense of the trauma and hurt inflicted on my young heart. Neither could she. I had no one to relieve the hurt. Neither did she. I took it all and carefully folded it up and tucked it away. I began to protect myself from it ever happening again. So did she.

# CHAPTER 7

# *Victoria's Purpose and Mine*

*One day I was standing in line with Victoria at Costco. I saw her looking at two little girls sitting in the cart in front of us. One was probably three and her sister, one. Victoria was looking at them sadly, which is the look she always has when no one is talking to her or she sees happy children. I wondered what she was thinking...I know what I was thinking...when she was one, she definitely wasn't sitting in a grocery cart shopping with her mom, gabbing and smiling to the person behind them in line. As I so naturally smiled at someone else's little girl, I looked at mine. My smile doesn't come so naturally to her. I called her over to my side and put my arm around her and held her close. She laid her head into the side of my leg. Nothing was going to move her. She needs my love. I need hers.*

There were many personal and heart-wrenching moments that I had to go through to get myself to a place where I was willing and able to provide Victoria a safe atmosphere to develop trust with some consistency. What was being required of me went against anything my heart had ever known. I did not want to set myself up for heartache. Who does? But I knew that my sincerity demanded vulnerability. It didn't really matter if Victoria's vindictiveness was coming from a destructive place or a place of protection; to a sensitive heart, it feels identical. As I began to understand her motivations, it helped me become less reactionary and demanding, but it hurt all the same.

Yet, I had to open myself up to Victoria to build trust with her. I worked hard for this. I worked hard to be able to understand her despite what she was saying. I had to put my best face on and allow her to push me to the edge over and over again so she could see I was here to stay. I had to be patient reacting to nothing. I couldn't hold onto grudges. I couldn't let her wear me down. I had to let her know I accepted her in whatever she decided to do. I often told her it was okay to be angry. It wasn't okay to be mean. Eventually, she did begin to trust me. In fact, I think she found some guilty pleasure knowing that she could treat me as badly as she could and yet, I would still love her the same. "Why do you still love me?" she would ask in disbelief. I answered her confidently, hiding *my* disbelief, "Because you deserve it."

When we first started therapy and held Victoria accountable for every one of her defiant behaviors, all day long my time was spent going head to head with her perfunctory moves and all the pain that it invoked. Although it was exhausting and she was taking all of my time, I was relieved to finally be in control of her and of me. As time progressed, she began to relinquish some control. We were still on the rollercoaster ride, but I was no longer throwing up over the side. The lows were getting a bit further apart, giving me a small reprieve.

Spending so much time trying to improve Victoria's behavior, and already struggling to show her affection, made it very difficult for me to maintain balance between love and logic. The logical part—to hold her responsible for everything—came easily. The love did not. I had to allow her to take my love, spit in my face (figuratively this time), feel her destroy my love, and then provide her with more the next morning. She talked about destroying it so effortlessly and emotionlessly. She told me she wanted to smash my love under the house and ride over it with her bike. I don't know how much of this talk was sincere. I wanted to have her think of ways she could take care of my love and feel it but I didn't want to waste my breath. I felt like I had wasted a lot of breaths. Even though I tried not to take her berating personally, I still internalized some of it. There were moments when I responded to her perfectly and there were moments when the best I conjured up did nothing to promote healing. Even though she often told me she didn't need my love and my mind wanted to believe her, my heart knew everyone, especially Victoria, longed to be loved.

Victoria began to be truthful with me, which I appreciated after years of her trying to say the right thing and living with one contradiction after another; but if her lies had battered me, the truth was crucifying.

She always wanted to talk about her negative feelings. Those were the ones she was most in touch with. As her trust in me began to strengthen, she felt free to share her sincere feelings. Unfortunately for me, most of these initial feelings were so damaging—so much hate and anger. One evening after a difficult day with Victoria, I convinced myself to read her a cuddle time book. I read one of my favorites because it reflected us both. It is called *Mama, Do You Love Me?* What I didn't realize was that the scary, dark side of Victoria was about to expose itself. I had always felt it. I didn't usually hear it.

The book is all about a daughter wondering and a mother confirming that she will still love her daughter even if she does mean things to her. I reached the page where the daughter turns into a polar bear, "the meanest bear you ever saw." This bear chases her mother into the tent, scaring her and making her cry. Victoria smiled as I read this part. This was typical behavior for Victoria that I usually ignored, but I decided to ask her if she liked that part. She said she liked that the girl was scared. I told her that was the mom. She smiled even bigger.

So I just thought and asked her, "Is there ever a time when you feel like the polar bear and want to get your mom and make her cry?"

"Yes," she said, "but there are more times when I don't."

"When do you not feel like the polar bear?" I asked.

"When you cuddle me, when you give me treats, when you let me go to my friend's house."

I said, "Do you know what the polar bear would do if she got the mom?"

"Yes," she said. "Kill her."

"Do you ever feel like killing me?" I tentatively asked.

"Yes."

"How often?" I questioned.

"Every day," came her quick reply.

"How many times a day?" I wondered.

"About twenty," she said effortlessly. "But I would be sad if you died," she said unconvincingly.

"Have you thought about how you would kill me?" I morbidly wondered.

"Yes, with a knife behind my back. I would sneak up and put it right in your stomach. Then I would put you in a suitcase."

This was one of the smoothest conversations we had ever had. "You would go to Heaven, wouldn't you?" she wondered.

"Yes," I calmly replied.

"How would you if you are in the suitcase?" she pondered.

"My spirit would go and then later my body. I don't know. Heavenly Father will take care of it," I answered in amazement.

"I could also take a big rock and throw it at your forehead and put you in a tiny closet. Or I would use scissors. Or just throw things at you," she continued. "I would kill the whole family so I could have Finn (our dog). I would take his tiny cage, his toys, and for sure his leash. We couldn't live alone so I would go live at my friend's house," she finished.

Thankfully. I was done with this conversation. I didn't even know where to go with it. I simply picked up the book, finished it, and tucked her in. Throughout the entire conversation I was composed and unruffled which is exactly what she needed me to be. If I would had shown her any fear or shock she would have known that I couldn't handle what was inside of her. Although this exchange was not totally unexpected, as I left the room my hands began to shake and I felt like I had just walked out of a bad dream. I felt sick and sad. These destructive thoughts, including killing, are not unusual in RAD children. She *thought* of picking up a knife, but many RAD kids actually do it. These murderous fantasies have more to do with a means to an end, that Victoria believes she will gain control than malicious intent. So I was not surprised that we had this conversation, but nothing could have prepared me for it. Almost the whole time I sat talking to her, I was imagining these words coming out of my other seven-year-old's mouth. It would never happen. I couldn't make total sense of the exchange we'd just had, but I knew I needed to share it with someone ASAP! I told Jay and he was very upset.

Jay was so upset that I knew I couldn't tell him about any more of the disturbing experiences I had with Victoria. He didn't want to hear them

> *"Pain changes us but not the same way healing teaches us. Healing can help us become more sensitive and awake to life."*
> —Elaine S. Marshall

and he had a hard time handling them. I spoke to Max about this and he explained that it was important for Victoria to share these stories, but I shouldn't ask for specifics unless she offers them. And while I wasn't so much concerned about Victoria harming me, I did worry about my children. We locked away all the knives and any other potential weapons.

I learned from this exchange that she was entrusting me and seeing if she could feel safe expressing herself. It also led me to ask Max to begin more intense therapy.

I wanted to share this story with others because it gave credence to what I had felt from Victoria from the beginning but nobody else could see. I thought it would prove to people that Victoria was really broken and that

I suffer the emotional effects of a damaged soul and destructive mind. But the story really never served that purpose for the people I told. It only scared the hell out of them. And rightly so.

Later I would learn in therapy with Max what Victoria was really trying to say in these harmful stories. They really had everything to do with being scared to love us and her fear that we would give up on her. If she could just get rid of us before we get rid of her, she could have the dog and decide where she lived. This time she would get to choose a friend's house and not end up in an orphanage. It was Victoria testing our love, tests she put us through over and over again. For years.

The Sunday before the *Mama, Do You Love Me* incident, we had sent Victoria to her room as a last resort. She was angry. When I went to check on her she was sitting on the floor. She was looking down at her ankle. I follow her eyes and saw a bloody foot. I was worried and quickly asked her what happened. "I was picking a scab," she replied. I didn't believe her. I looked around because it appeared that she'd been cut by a piece of glass. I washed the wound off and put a Band-aid on it. I tried not to make a big deal about it, but asked her what happened and why she would want to pick her scab so badly. "I wanted to see myself bleed," she replied. She did these things to herself at other times on a smaller scale. We had not yet started seeing Max again, and while I knew this all had to do with coping or trying to feel, I had no idea how to respond. She had shared enough destructive thoughts with me—hurting, killing, breaking, smashing, ripping, and cutting. I knew someday if she didn't get help, she would become more physically aggressive.

Anger is a secondary emotion, which means there is always an underlying catalyst. Why was she so angry? Most of the anger stemmed from the hurt of abandonment followed by the injustice of a loveless orphanage and consequent abuse and neglect. Added by the frustration of adoptive parents who couldn't help and made things worse. She was also angry about what was required of her, which was so hard, and confused by a mind that didn't want to let her do the right thing. She was fighting a battle daily to free her heart. She didn't even know she had a heart at war. It's the only heart she has ever known. That sounded eerily familiar to me. This was the exact journey I was on. She was trying to free her heart of the very same things I was, so that her capacity to feel love and express empathy would increase.

I don't know who could understand the pain I have felt except for Victoria. And I was raised in a home with parents and siblings that loved me. She was a lone orphan in an institution. Five thousand miles away our paths crossed and we helped each other fix what we could not fix alone. Our similarities included a lack of nurturing, being victims of circumstances we had no control over, relying on ourselves because we didn't have anyone to help us understand, and being taken advantage of. The result of these things is the reflection of me I see in her. We lacked trust, we found it hard to empathize, and exerted an enormous amount of control to protect ourselves from becoming victims again. I struggled with issues of trust and self-worth, especially concerning appearance and confidence. I had every opportunity to screw it all up. Drugs, drinking, smoking, promiscuity, and shoplifting were all easy outs falsely promising comfort and relief. But I didn't take that route. What saved me from a lifetime of anger and destruction was that I had developed a strong moral conscience and secure foundation of faith. Additionally, a few people in my life with unconditional love and stability saved me from further heartache.

It is the same strength that came from my faith in an abiding and loving God that enabled me to trust enough to accept the help from Max as he encouraged me to free my heart to help Victoria's. It wasn't easy. It *had* to be hard. I needed the confidence of knowing I could do the difficult things required of me so that I could survive more challenges with Victoria. I have never felt the Refiner's fire in progress. Usually, it is subtle and clear with hindsight, but then I felt it daily, molding me into something better and stronger. Those hard days didn't make me weak at the seams. They forged me for what lay ahead.

*These last few months haven't even been about her. It has been about getting myself to a place where I can help her. And that wasn't even clear. That took six months of battering Max and living with so much frustration to figure out. I have just felt I have taken the long road to Nowhere. Twice. But here I am walking down the road to Somewhere. I refuse to end up in Nowhere again. I am afraid. I am uncertain. I am inviting healing, but expecting pain. I am walking a demanding road with a comforting Guide.*

I am blessed to understand the purpose of Victoria in my life. With perfect timing (which happened on more than one occasion), Max gave me a book to read called *The Little Soul and the Sun* by Neale Donald Walsh. It is about a small soul that wants to become who he really is by becoming forgiving. The only way to do that would require a "friendly soul," an angel, who would do something to him so he could develop this attribute. An angel was willing to help the Little Soul become all he could be because she loved him. But she only had one request.

Walsh writes, "In the moment that I strike you and smite you," the Friendly Soul replied, "in the moment that I do the worst to you that you could possibly imagine—in that very moment..."

"Yes?" the Little Soul interrupted, "yes...?"

The Friendly Soul became quieter still.

"Remember who I really Am."

"Oh, I will!" cried the Little Soul, "I promise! I will always remember you as I see you right here, right now!"

"Good," said the Friendly Soul, "because, you see, I will have been pretending so hard, I will have forgotten myself. And if you do not remember me as I really am, I may not be able to remember for a very long time. And if I forget Who I Am, you may even forget Who You Are, and we will both be lost. Then we will need another Soul to come along and remind us both of Who We Are."

"No, we won't!" the Little Soul promised again. "I will remember you! And I will thank you for bringing me this gift—the chance to experience myself as Who I Am."

These are sacred words. I have no doubt that before Victoria and I arrived on this earth, we had a similar exchange. We promised each other to help fulfill the measure of our creation on this earth. I must admit I nearly forgot who I was and I wasn't able to see her for who she was. I did need another Soul or two and a Savior to remind me. I am so glad I was paying attention and that they were so willing.

I was talking to Victoria one night four years after she came to America and I told her, "You are so lucky that you have a mom and a dad who are helping you fix your broken heart. I had a broken heart just like yours and I didn't have anyone to help me for a long time."

"When did you find help?" she asked.

"In February," I replied.

"What?! When you were thirty-six?" she asked in shock.

"Yes," I said.

"I am NOT waiting until I am thirty-six," she spoke emphatically.

"No," I smiled. "I don't want you to. But I know it's hard. I know what it feels like," I sincerely confirmed.

This is why I take it so seriously because it is so serious. And I feel an enormous amount of pressure as the one who will help her get better. I also take it seriously because I have to work so hard for everything that is required of me. Being forgiving, patient, nurturing, unconditional, encouraging, and sensitive doesn't come easy for me. It is much easier now and while I may not be the best mom for this job, I am the only. Thankfully the Lord makes up for my meager offerings and attempts.

# CHAPTER 8

# *Heart In The Right Place*

*After years of feeling like her enemy, I now knew
I had to be Victoria's advocate. I knew that people
around me, including Jay, weren't going to be able to
understand her complexities. I knew that the way
I treated her set a precedent for everyone around me.*

*I* grew stronger. I was still the pincushion taking all the jabs. It was painful but I wasn't hanging onto it. I understood and felt sorry for Victoria. I saw it wasn't so much about disobeying me, as it was hard for Victoria to trust and let go of the misery even though it took more effort for her to maintain the despair. So my heart hurt for her wrong choices, but I was not hurt personally by the disobedience. Finally.

Freeing my heart of the trauma that was holding me back allowed me to let love in and become able to move forward with Victoria. It allowed me to feel for her and begin to understand her. I had needed this clarity for so long. I realized that not only was her love dependent on attention but on tangible things as well. It was this that made going into her room at night after a difficult day and offering her a piece of candy all the more arduous. I knew that the candy was making her happy. It wasn't me. I wanted it to be about me more than the candy. Really, that's all I've ever wanted. I've wanted her to love me not the drink, not the food, not the toy, not the neighbor, not the swimming. Just me, no matter what.

I used a suggestion given to us by another therapist to draw a heart on my hand instead of giving Victoria chocolate. I felt so good about it because my love was so much more than candy. So, as I walked into the room, the first thing she did was stare at my clasped hand. I asked her what she thought was in it and she responded with some crazy answer that would never fit in my hand. Then I asked her again and she said, "Chocolate." I opened my hand with all sincerity and said, "No, it's my love." To say she was disappointed was an understatement. But I didn't mind. I knew deep down she wanted my love, but her damaged mind still told her she wanted things, wanted chocolate. I continued to do this and then one night before leaving her room, I decided to draw my heart on her hand. That was meaningful to her. I saw her eyes light up, but more than that, after I shut the door I could hear her saying, "Mom's heart is on my hand." Over and over.

It was interesting. It used to be that when I implemented a consequence I would want her to suffer for it, and the more, the better. It doesn't work that way. It only made her angrier. One day when her cousins were visiting Victoria wasn't allowed to play with them. I knew if I left her to her own devices, the anger would build and she would just think about killing me, feel like a victim, hang on to the grudge, and plan how she would pay me back for not letting her play. So I wanted to do something to get her away from the house. I wanted to take her to the candy store, share a milk shake with her, or buy her a book. That was too simple. It took a lot more creativity and more of me to encourage her to feel my love. I couldn't do it with things. So I took her to the park and pushed her on the swing and played games. I reminded her that I was showing her love (I have to point out my love to her all the time) but she was too selfish and thought it had everything to do with her. What she didn't realize was that I was distracting her from the demons that sabotaged her thoughts when she became angry. This is still hard for me because I want her to be sorry, not angry, but I am the target and the distraction. Talk about being pulled in too many different directions!

I finally found myself not only being sensitive to Victoria but even protective of her. It got easier to see her for who she was and not what I wanted her to be. *Acceptance.* It got easier not take things personally and seek to understand her. *Empathy.* It got easier to not to become so anxious. *Patience.* And it wasn't everyday, but it was so different from anything I had felt since she had left Belarus and that was so promising.

With my understanding of how she was not appreciative of my love (she didn't see it or feel it) and now being in a position to offer her more, I committed the cardinal sin of mothers with RAD children: I withdrew Victoria from school.

I held Victoria back a year so she started kindergarten when she was seven during the fall we came back from Ireland. School had been a source of contention since she started, but I was only now recognizing the source of that and finally in a place to do something about it. Victoria had gone to a year of preschool. I knew she was getting loads of attention and treats but I wasn't willing to fight for that attention, and frankly, I needed the break from her. When kindergarten started I was hesitant tell the teacher about the problems we had with Victoria. I really felt like it was between my daughter and me. I also didn't want to bring up concerns if the teacher wasn't ever going to see them, and I ran the risk of her not understanding anyway. The new, strict boundaries at home immediately created security for Victoria, although she tested them relentlessly. When she started school she was thrown into the ocean without a life preserver and it was unfair for me to not provide her teacher with one.

At school it was hard for Victoria to keep her head above water when she was trying to interact with other children, have freedom she couldn't channel, and relinquish control to a teacher who didn't have the upper hand. It was an impossible situation. The minute school started, any progress that we had made reached a plateau or regressed. She no longer tried to earn my trust and love when she could get attention at school to fulfill that superficial need. What I didn't know and wouldn't know until six weeks after school started was that Victoria struggled in the classroom. She was trying to control the teacher and she was alienating herself from the other students.

I sat down at parent teacher conference and ask her teacher, "How is Victoria?"

"How do you think she is doing?" the teacher replied.

"I have no idea," I returned.

*Negative attention was easier to give mainly because that was what she demanded most and on the surface seemed to deserve, but only until you looked past it all, underneath the wellness of her face and remembered how sick she was. It had taken me so long to get to this place where I can see all her motivations come from one damaged heart and mind.*

"She is struggling," her teacher revealed. "She won't follow directions, she doesn't share, and she hasn't made any friends. She is very subtle. She cuts other kids' paper. She cuts her own hair. I know I am exhausted by her at the end of the day."

My first thought was regret that I hadn't spoken to the teacher. Anyone who had that much contact with her needed to be in the know. I then felt, not relief, not comfort, but something substantial realizing that it wasn't me. This wasn't about Victoria and me. This was about Victoria. It was about whomever was in charge of her and the longer you were with her, the more likely you were to see her selfish, manipulative behaviors.

I had Max meet with her kindergarten teacher after this conference to give a brief overview of RAD, offer some solutions, and answer questions. I really believed her teacher understood Victoria; she simply didn't have the time to deal with all her behaviors, especially if they weren't disrupting the classroom. I had to ask her to ignore many of the behaviors. For example, when she would tell the students to put their pencils down, Victoria wouldn't. She would ask the students to write the letter "A" and Victoria would intentionally not put the line across. Little, incessant offenses all day long. The teacher fed into them because they seemed so miniscule but her teacher began to be worn down. I needed the teacher to ignore this, and that was challenging. Then the more obvious problems: hitting other kids, talking, being bossy and selfish with the other children, needed very consistent consequences. But the consequences never came. Victoria worked the system charmingly. There were cards with different colors to signify the consequence—first given a warning, then miss recess, then see the principal. Well, Victoria knew nothing would happen with the first card so she pushed it every day. Then she began to realize if her second card was pulled they sometimes forgot to have her miss recess or they wouldn't follow through.

I had asked the school to withhold treats from Victoria and that was a major source of contention. They couldn't understand how that was affecting the relationship I had with her.

There were so many things at school hindering our progress at home. For instance, Victoria knew I helped her with homework on my terms. She was sent home at the beginning of each month with a task card to be completed by the end of the month. There were times when she wouldn't get the card done because of choices she made. She would go to school and tell her teacher, "My mom won't help me with my task card, she is too busy." So, the teacher took Victoria to the phone and called me. I was not home but Victoria got so much satisfaction from controlling her teacher and making me defend myself. The teacher thought Victoria was lying but still called. I told her teacher I don't mind her calling but I did mind her letting Victoria stand there while she did it.

There was another occasion which I should have seen coming: Victoria was sent to school without breakfast or a treat. Treats were/are such a sore subject for me with her. She is obsessed with making sure she has a treat in the morning to take to school. It was becoming a power struggle, so for a while we stopped sending them but then she began to harass the students for theirs. Reluctantly, we began sending them again. One morning she was dragging getting up, getting dressed, and cleaning her room. I warned her she was running out of time to eat breakfast. She didn't finish, missed her breakfast and became very angry. She then began to question me about her snack. I told her I knew what was best for her. Right before we left I went to put a treat in her bag and saw there was one already there. She sheepishly denied putting it there so I took it out and sent her without one. I explained she would be hungry but she would not starve to death. I should have known she would go directly to the teacher and tell her she was hungry. This time it was worse. The teacher had Victoria call me and say, "Mom, Mrs. Patterson wants to know why you didn't feed me breakfast and won't let me have a treat." I was livid. I was so angry that Victoria was given control—the teacher caved. If I had been thinking clearly I would have had Victoria explain it all but I didn't want to say one more word to her. I asked to speak with her teacher. After,

I had explained, the teacher replied again that she suspected as much. I thought, "If she suspected Victoria of being controlling, I wished she wouldn't have responded to it."

These are just a couple of obvious instances. They don't begin to convey the multiple seemingly insignificant occurrences that happened throughout the day when the teacher overlooked or missed Victoria's actions all together. She was also getting attention at school through hugs, candy—all the different ways she internalized attention as affection. I was getting suspicious looks from the teacher's aide who believed she needed to provide Victoria with everything it appeared she wasn't getting at home. This was a familiar response to me, even from my own family members. I knew it was difficult to understand from the outside looking in, but the suspicion was hurtful. Other people thought they could provide what I seemed to be withholding. So did I, once upon a time. *She just needs more love.* I have loved this child more than anyone despite what I could not do for her. This love brought her to our home. This love allowed her to stay. This love will mend her. This love will allow her to love others. And despite what outsiders thought, they had not seen her love.

So as hard as it was, for me, it was the right thing to do to pull her out of the last few months of school. What it simply came down to was this: I couldn't compete with anyone else. I would always lose to the shallowness of attention. Victoria always chose the schoolteacher, the Sunday School teacher, the smiling stranger primarily because they were unsuspecting. She could engage them and not have to give anything in return. My love was scary to her. My love wanted to give *and* take. Plus, there weren't many negative reactions outside the home. She was unlikely to receive consequences for bad behavior, although she would gladly take that attention too. If she could find someone with whom she could get away with her passiveness, she preferred it over home. I had to set myself up for success here, which meant I had to remove any competition or distractions. I needed her to prefer me. I needed to do everything I could to make sure I wouldn't be pushed back by her again and to show her I did love her no matter what; because until she attached truly and deeply to me she'd never have the ability to connect to anybody else.

I was not perfect. I knew I would mess up. I would become impatient. I would let old feelings reemerge unintentionally. Yet now I had more understanding, more resolve, and a heart that had a greater capacity to love. And not just her.

When we first started therapy I had been depleted. The insight and help Max provided in the first couple of months made such a significant difference in our lives. I wasn't feeling confident in knowing what to do with Victoria based on my past history of complicating things. I hung onto his every word. I had some preconceived notions about therapists. Let's just say they were pretty lofty. Max had some challenges that would not allow him to ever live up to these standards. I think it has to do with him being human or something—and that he had to deal with me. I expected the rest of therapy to continue evolving at the initial pace and with that understanding. That wasn't how it worked.

We had taken about three months off of therapy when we began again. I had a much better understanding and perspective on how it all worked. No therapist has all the answers. They have their best guess based on past history. Sometimes it worked, sometimes it didn't. But the greatest lesson I learned was that I could know what is best for Victoria. I was entirely confident in myself and my intent with her. I felt like I could make suggestions to Max. I believed I could decide whether or not something would work. That was important. I lived with her 24/7. I had insights no one else had. And I trusted myself. It is amazing what happens when your heart is in the right place.

# CHAPTER 9

# *Breaking Down Victoria's Emotional Fortress*

*I want all my efforts to be received with sincerity and responded to with love. That is my hope. And my hope for Victoria is to have a fun, happy, light hearted, and carefree life— exactly the way it should be for any child.*

Victoria's behaviors started to improve after I took her out of school. However, hearing more damaging thoughts from her, Victoria needed to start therapy again. That was when Max informed me we were just beginning the second half, her emotions. This, he assured me, would be more difficult for Victoria. I think he really meant for both of us. Jay no longer attended these therapy sessions, but I was so thankful he was there nearly every week for the previous sessions. It was important for him to understand the process so we could be on the same page when disciplining and responding to Victoria. She needed that consistency. There were times when it was easier for Jay to be the disciplinarian and that left me to take care of the nurturing. Since he was at so many sessions, he had a good understanding of it all. And Jay was good at offering humorous one-liners when my intensity instigated too much seriousness. That happened, and happens, often.

Jay looked at me around this time and said in all sincerity, "If something happened to you, I don't know what would happen to her." This is one time I knew he wasn't kidding. The journey to heal Victoria is really between her and me. If I could get her to trust and love me, she could then form bonds with others. Jay was my rock. He provided an enormous amount of stability through his constant support, encouragement, and love for me. This really was my battle, but this was his perspective:

*I began to get frustrated at her constant and seemingly deliberate actions. I put a camera in her room watching her and wanting her responsible for all of her actions. But I can see now we were just feeding into her need for attention. For the first two years I wasn't as aware as Jodi but I would take Victoria and provide Jodi relief. It took me a while to understand the complexities.*

*It used to be easy for me to cuddle and play with Victoria, but during the past year, even as we gained understanding, it has been difficult for me. I think it all has to do with seeing and understanding her direct attacks on Jodi.*

*Victoria has kind of held the family hostage. She demands so much of our time and we can't always do things together if she's losing privileges or acting out. If she misses out on things, she definitely wants the whole family to suffer for it. She tries to direct everyone and thinks she knows what is best. She takes up most of the conversations between Jodi and I.*

*There has never been enough trust with her to treat her as a normal kid or do things with friends. She rarely earns the privilege to go play downstairs. I wish we could enjoy her playing at the park, riding her bike, playing soccer, or taking dance. She seems to take fun things and turn them into a chore.*

*It was helpful to attend therapy with Jodi for a year. I felt like it was my duty to bring humor into the sessions. The understanding we received from Max helped us connect the dots to figure Victoria out and what to do with her.*

*My advice to husbands is to be supportive and allow the mother time away from the child, especially in the evenings and on the week-*

*end. It was important to spend time with other children as Victoria became so demanding.*

*I still struggle with responding to Victoria. I have a hard time ignoring her need for control and fall victim to feeding into her annoying behaviors. I still react to her at times and it just fuels the fire. When she feels bad, I want her to feel worse. The only time I feel compassionate is when she is sensitive after expressing real emotion and I can't feel the hate from her. She is like a rudderless airplane, no control.*

We decided to bring in another therapist to work with Max as we tried to break down Victoria's emotional walls. I was now ready for more intense therapy. The time was right. I had no idea what was going to go on in that room for 120 minutes. I didn't know what to expect from these therapy sessions but Max warned me this was when trauma can resurface for the parent. I didn't need any more of that. I was still healing; my changes still trying to feel permanent, but I was ready. It was time to focus on Victoria again. I won't include all the aspects of these months but I will share the most important parts.

The first thing we talked to Victoria about was her birth story. I have come to learn that repeatedly telling her story to her helps her understand more about herself. As I continue to share and she continues to mature, she will make sense of it in different ways. I recall this conversation about two years after she first came home.

"Mom, I wasn't born in anyone's tummy," Victoria said.

I looked at her surprisingly and said, "Of, course you were. Everyone was born in somebody's tummy. You weren't born in mine but you did have a mother that carried you in her tummy."

Victoria believed she existed in the orphanage and had always been there. I imagine she had spent plenty of time forming self-protection from this knowledge. I told her, as I have told her before, about her birth mother.

I told her when she was born her birth mother had two other children and didn't have enough things to take care of a newborn baby. Most of her pain and suffering comes from this act of abandonment. These conversations made it painful, but it was eventually healing. I know.

Max initially focused on her anger about her birth mother. He used all kinds of techniques, such as: psychodrama, objects relations theory, behavioral theory, and reverse psychology. Victoria was very aware of her angry feelings and could articulate them. She was just like any of us—finding it hard to go to those painful places and express true emotion. We were doing two hour sessions, two or three days a week. And some days, after two excruciating hours, she revealed nothing. These therapy sessions were pushing Victoria to take down her walls. She fought and we pushed. It was demanding. She was hard. I hated spending two hours and getting nowhere. I noticed in these sessions, even if she didn't break, it broke me. It was interesting. I just sat quietly on the couch for two hours, yet I walked out feeling like I had been beaten with a baseball bat. Hurt flowed from her, from crevices in my past, to what could be but wasn't, and many of the conversations and tactics were the exact things I had done when Victoria first came home. I was trying to calm her fears, hold her in my arms, and find some relief in me. It evoked stress and trauma revisiting those moments. And it was often my struggle. Alone. This was between her and me. Some days it felt like I was losing the battle. But I had this faith that would not allow me to accept defeat. I wanted to hold up the white flag nearly everyday. I could think of a million reasons why I should. And one reason why I couldn't. I loved her more than I even knew. It is this love that encouraged me to keep showing up amidst the doubt, fear, and urge to cancel.

Victoria was starting to feel me. My sincerity. My consistency. My love. It was scaring her. She was raging more often but not everyday which Max told me to expect. But I saw the progress in it. Therapy was breaking down walls. S-l-o-w-l-y.

In the sessions when she opened up, I gained more insight into her and felt more of her. It increased my sensitivity to her. I needed that. In one of

*Victoria is trying to obey. She is finding some value in obedience, which I appreciate as the only source of love she shows; and that isn't even consistent. Her love is still very volatile and conditional on what's in it for her.*

the more profound sessions she named all the reasons she was mad at her birth mother. The specific way in which she voiced each reason reminded me of her behaviors when we first brought her home. I could see that all the anger she had for her birth mother was directed at me. Max drew a face on the whiteboard representing her birth mother, as she released her anger, he slowly erased it.

She screamed at the white board, "I am mad at you because you didn't want me!" I could feel her saying to me, *You won't want me either.*

She screamed, "I am mad at you because you didn't feed me!" I could feel her saying, *You won't want to feed me either.*

"I am mad at you because you left me in a crib all day long!" *You will want to leave me in my room all day long.*

"I am mad at you because you gave me away because I was bad!" *You will think I am bad too.*

"I am mad that you loved your other kids more than me!" *You will love my brothers more than me.*

"I am mad that you kicked me!" *You will want to kick me.*

"I am mad that you didn't cuddle me!" *You won't want to cuddle me.*

"I am mad you didn't care how I felt!" *You won't care how I feel.*

"I am mad that you didn't think about me!" *You won't want to think about me.*

"I am mad that you never played with me." *You won't want to play with me.*

"I am mad you didn't give me anything." *You won't want to give me anything.*

She was right. I felt all of these feelings. Now I knew why. It was so important for me to learn where the majority of her anger came from and that all of her subtle behaviors were means to get me to react and confirm how she was feeling. I fell right into the trap. I knew my early reactions were digging a hole I didn't know how to get out of, but now I was climbing out. She finally reached a place where the emotion, anger for now, was so real and so big. It was humbling that I am her caregiver, responsible for someone so hurt and broken. Her revelations were nearly as freeing for me as they were for her. I wish I could have known sooner so I could have taken care of her with all the tenderness I have and had. Now I could help heal what I hurt. I could provide some redemptive work. I was glad that she was still here and I was still here. It was nothing short of a miracle.

At the end of each session I read Victoria a cuddle time book that was a story expressing love, typically between a mother and a child. When I went into therapy with an open heart, I was usually touched so that I could be sincere with my cuddling. At times it was still aching for me, but I knew each time it was healing for her.

During the following weeks, I found myself wondering if this is a "Get Mad at Birth Mom" game so we could fall in love with Mom. And I guess it kind of started out that way with all of Victoria's nervousness and smiles, touching my hair, and kissing my hand. But who was I to be judgmental about expressing true emotion? Her trying often seemed better than my doing. It wasn't a game but it is was so orchestrated. I wrestled with that but realized most of my other efforts never resulted in sincerity.

One day Victoria and Max scribbled out anger on a piece of paper, waded it up, screamed into it, naming what the anger was, and threw it across the room. I watched them as they both did this and two feelings encompassed me. I felt an enormous amount of gratitude for Max and an equal amount of sadness for Victoria. My sadness wasn't just about the amount the anger. I was sad she had lived with it her entire life but couldn't identify it. She couldn't name it. I didn't even know. How could she? She could now. And we have thought of many different ways for her to redirect her anger. Her mind cleared when she let go of the mad. She became childlike and seemingly for the moment, carefree. It was refreshing. We drove home from therapy that day and she was in the back talking like a happy child. She was pretending she had a soccer game and needed to get home before four o'clock. We were having a fun conversation. She was entertaining and using her imagination. I didn't even know she had one that didn't include inflicting pain. On the way home I asked her to do a few things before she went out and played her pretend soccer game, but when we arrived she went directly to the front yard. I sensed she was sabotaging herself again. I let her know she needed to tell her pretend coach she wouldn't be able to go the soccer game. She got angry. Yes, it was that swift. But I saw this was a great opportunity for her to go yell out her mad. I had her jump on the mini tramp. She was jumping, naming it, and letting it go. While she was jumping I was talking on the phone and Jay was leaving and took Victoria with him. I called her later and told her I was sorry I didn't get to talk to her. "Do you still have mad?" I asked having no expectations. "No, it's gone," said the happy, lighthearted voice I was not used to hearing. I needed no other convincing. Without even thinking, "I love you" slipped from my lips…and my heart.

We continued to address the mad in Victoria's life, which included but definitely was not limited to her birth mother, me, Jay, her brothers, and Max. That kept her busy for a while and it was working. I noticed very quickly that she wasn't as easily provoked. She still got mad and mean, but it wasn't rage. And it wasn't all the time.

I never knew what Max's agenda was when I arrived for therapy. He really didn't either until he began to talk to me, we evaluated the week, and then he spoke with Victoria. Worse than not having an agenda was not knowing how the sessions were going to affect me. On one occasion, Max had me hold Victoria and he began to prompt Victoria to ask me the following questions:

"Will you ever stop loving me?"

"Will you always keep me safe?"

"Will you ever give up on me?"

"Will you always look for me if I am lost?"

"Will you always shelter me from the storms?"

I understood the importance of comforting her fears. I didn't know if she was still scared of any of these things but she could have been. The things he began naming were the very things I struggled with that made me feel inadequate and guilty. I felt my trauma. I could respond confidently now.

Not easily, but with surety. It did bring up those times, not so long ago, that lasted longer than the confident ones I had now. I felt blindsided, but I knew I had to address those fears even though we never spoke about them because I knew she felt my insecurities. There was something else I knew I had to deal with and that was my good friend, guilt. I felt sorrow—deep sorrow for her beginning in life and her beginning in her second life. I didn't usually live with regrets. I had avoided them for most of my life or let them go, but there was one hanging on for dear life—my initial responses to Victoria were the opposite of everything I thought I was. That is why for so long I didn't even really know who I was. I was angry, mean, yelling, vindictive, depressed, anxious, and clinging onto control that was slipping away. I felt weak. I felt like I was everything I had vowed not to be. It was completely breaking my heart and my spirit. These responses to her and my quest for justification brought me to the depths of sorrow.

As soon as I began to learn the motivations behind her behaviors, the first thing I had to do was walk that everpersonal road of repentance and forgiveness. I, with miracles working in my heart, was able to completely forgive her for the things she was not even accountable for. I was able to let go of all the animosity and resentment. I did not hang onto any anger or justification. I had no idea how it was going to happen but it did. And that was the easy part—if there really was one.

I then had to seek forgiveness for myself and that God freely gave. The Spirit bore witness to me many times that my penance had been paid. Not only had I paid the price for my choices, my Savior had as well. Even with that knowledge, I could not let guilt go. The guilt that followed me would not let me go. I began to put conditions on when I would release the regret and accept the forgiveness. I would let it go when Victoria was better.

This served no purpose. In fact, she couldn't get better until my heart was free to help hers. It was personal. It was long in coming. It was sweet in releasing. Do I wish it had been different? Of course.

For so long I held onto the injustice that I felt from her. It would not allow me to do what needed to be done but I got there. I began to do the

Right before one therapy session ended, Max told Victoria that in the moments she feels like making a bad choice to ask for my love instead. The instant he said it, stress engulfed me. I thought to myself, "She still sneaks food because she won't ask for it. How is she going to ask me for my love?" And when I thought of her insatiable demands for love with passive-aggressive behaviors, it was nearly more than this weary heart could commit to. It didn't last very long. I just found her being mean to me soon after giving her loving attention. I knew she still couldn't trust it.

things required to help her build trust and love, but I only could get so far without letting go of my guilt. In releasing it, I was able to talk about those times and express my feelings and reactions, in the safe secure arms of mercy and love. I could tell her I was sorry; really mean it; and feel the redemption. Here is a journal entry from that time:

> *That day was today. I knew it was coming. I don't know if it healed me more than her. Everything in this experience has been about timing. His timing. And for a while now, I have been on the Lord's watch. Listening, feeling, and acting. I have had some help. And he has been listening, feeling, and acting. It has been a combined effort.*
>
> *What I did today was easy. Last week it would have been grueling. What a difference a day, or two, or three makes. It was tender. I didn't say everything I had wanted but I said everything I needed. I explained to Victoria that I thought I was prepared to bring her into our family. I wanted her here but when she came, she was mean and angry. "I tried so hard to love you until I became mean and angry. I couldn't figure it out. I didn't know what to do for you and I am sorry," I said. Victoria takes my face in her hands and says, "That's OK." I ask her if she remembers times when I was mean and angry. She can hardly remember and I can't forget. Max says this is typical. It's one of God's tender mercies protecting these children from further trauma. My boys have also been protected. I have always felt this. They had every reason to be resentful of a girl that turned our family upside down and demanded me in ways that should have left them wanting. They haven't. I thank God. I also thank my other half, Jay.*

As I have alluded, breaking through Victoria's wall was strenuous, time consuming, and slow. We were constantly looking for that weakening in the fortress to have new, healing, and helpful moments with her. They were rare and short lived. Each day that passed gave me a better understanding of her and of me. I also understood that nothing would ever get any worse.

I had felt as bad as it gets. Of that I am completely sure. What I didn't know was the feeling of as good as it gets. I had a small, beautiful, healing, hopeful, personal, and LOVING moment with Victoria a few weeks into talking about her birth mother. We were just finishing two hours of intense therapy when the wall started to weaken. We got into the car to go home. I always sit for a moment to regain composure and write my feelings in those moments. She was in the back seat and she continued to talk about her feelings. I could see she was still "in the zone" and real feelings were being manifested. I put away my notebook and sat her on the center console between the two front seats so I could see her face. She was being so vulnerable. We were looking at each other. I dare say, our hearts were welcoming each other. I felt an overwhelming amount of sensitivity towards her. I brought her into the front seat, held her in my arms, and spoke to her, for the first time, heart to heart. I can't remember all the words that were said that day, but of this I am sure—it was divine. It was as real and pure as it gets. Just trying to think of the specific words feels like it would somehow diminish the experience, but this is what I remember most:

"Mom," Victoria said to me in astonishment, "I am mad and sad at my birth mom." She said this to me over and over. Her revelation of the hurt and anger she had for her birth mom was freeing. She had lived her lifetime with this anger without knowing where it came from. Neither had I. She had taken it out on me for four years because she didn't know how to get rid of it. And neither did I.

"Why did she give me away? Why didn't she give one of her other kids away?" she grieved.

"I don't know, Victoria," I told her. "I don't think we will ever know exactly why. But there are only two things you need to know. One, is that she gave you away and two, it hurts a lot."

As I said this tears, real tears, swelled up in her eyes. She fought them and I knew exactly what that felt like.

"It does hurt," she bravely confided.

"I know. Does it hurt right here?" I asked as I touched her chest.

"Yes," her voice cracked, "it hurts all over."

"How big is the hurt?" I asked.

Victoria turned her head slightly to look out the front window, "Do you see the sky?"

"Yes," I answered.

"Do you see how big it is? And how it never ends?"

"Yes," my voice cracked.

"That's how much it hurts," she safely confided. Allowing her to feel and understand the hurt she has endured is more than a small heart should ever have to bear.

"I am sorry, Victoria. I'm trying to help you so that we can help the hurt go away," I spoke with all the love I had.

"I am so glad I have you," she said with all the love she had.

Beautiful, healing words were exchanged for forty-five minutes. I put her in the back seat of the car and she said, for the first time, "Mom, I feel your love."

"How do you know?" I asked.

"Because it feels so good," she said excitedly.

"What does it feel like?" I wondered.

"It feels better than swimming. It feels better than ice cream."

And I know she genuinely felt my love but even more importantly, for the first time ever, I felt hers. For the first time since bringing her home, I felt fortunate to be her mother. In those moments, I saw what it was in me that made me the only one who could do this for her and that could survive her. I didn't want to let her out of my sight. I wanted to hang onto her. I wanted this day to stay. It was the sincerity I had been waiting four years for. It wasn't a sword. It was the Balm of Gilead.

Victoria maintained this new fine for a day. Jay couldn't believe the transformation. I could hardly believe it. I was so excited the following day to tell Max about this truly pivotal moment. I recounted the story and told him, "Max, I really feel like she could have asked me to do anything for her in that moment. I would have done it. Anything."

"That's awesome," he sincerely replied.

"Is this the change we have been waiting for? Is this the light switch that has just been flipped and will stay on?" I eagerly pleaded.

He looked at me gently and explained, "It's a wonderful moment to come back to but it's only a step."

"I don't believe it. It felt too good to the both of us. We will maintain it," I promised.

Max only looked at me doubtfully, "If it could happened to anyone it would be you. But it would be a first."

I didn't let that affect me. After the redefining moment in the car, the exchanges in therapy, and the angel that showed up Friday morning. I really did convince myself she was here to stay. I was feeling hopeful. Too hopeful. I could maintain it. She couldn't.

This disappointment of seeing Victoria slip away knows no words. It unfortunately expressed itself in anger. The ease in which I felt justified in my anger brought me back to the early days when we were both operating under massive amounts of rage. My imperfections were shining through. This was the same anger that was resentful by the vulnerability of it all. This hurt; hurt like carelessness. This hurt, hurt like I couldn't ever do enough good. I was so careful this time not to take it out on her that everyone else bore the brunt of it, but forgivingly. I was blessed to have people who love and trust in who I really was and not my imperfections.

While I couldn't protect myself from the hurt and disappointment, I could protect myself from my anger that ensued. But it was so swift. I didn't even feel like I had a choice. I was so sad I allowed myself to go back there so quickly and struggled to pull myself out of it. Who did this sound like? I have at times lived in her very world. I see the source of the anger. I saw what it was trying to do to me. I saw how Satan was trying to weaken me at my most sensitive seams. Those were the very seams the Lord and I had mended. But thankfully they are stronger than before.

There were no guarantees at any given time that Victoria would let down her guard and allow me in, but the few times she had, she allowed me to see her for who she really was, and witness the good and love that she had to offer. And it was so sweet and tender. Angelic. I can remember using that word and it surprised me now, because it used to be that with her, angelic was the furthest thing from my mind.

I'm not the perfect mom to Victoria. I recognize that I know her needs and understand her thinking most of the time. I am still impatient; yet I know I am doing most things right after doing most things wrong for so long. So I don't beat myself up, I just try to focus on the steady but slow progress.

# CHAPTER 10

# *Painful And Slow Progress*

*There are many moments now where Victoria looks fine.*
*Not a loving, attached fine, not a happy-ending fine. Just*
*fine. And I wish just fine were good enough. I wish just*
*fine would satisfy my heart. I could live with just fine.*
*She would continue to struggle with just fine.*

When it came time for the next therapy session, Victoria was ready to go right back to those good feelings. I, of course, was tentative. Max said he would protect me that day. That was important to me but I knew it was only for that day. I knew thirty minutes into the session that he couldn't protect me for all the other days. When it came to cuddle time, I held Victoria but I would not look at her and allow her to go to those really loving, comforting places. It felt abusive. It was ripping my heart out. How do I know? Because I have endured it more times than I care to remember. And not just with her.

She was feeling good; but it was expressed in giddiness, not controlled like the day in the car. It was clearly a natural high, but it appeared to be almost drug-induced. In fact, I was a bit uncomfortable witnessing it in Max's office. She touched me and played with my hair. She told me I was beautiful, I was the best mom ever, and how much she loved me. I didn't have any control over it. And she didn't either. I knew she didn't know how to react to her good feelings, that she wasn't used to them, but just when I had gotten used to her taking my love and throwing it away, I now had to learn to let her take my love, wallow in it, experience it, and then throw it away. She still didn't appreciate or allow it to sustain her. This was

139

a pain I couldn't protect myself from. I couldn't choose to not take that personally. I couldn't do for her what needed to be done with any amount of protection. I could be careful but I couldn't construct any barriers.

So I then had to open myself up and let her take what she needed. I anticipated feelings of being abused, taken for granted, left alone, and depleted. But somehow in the depths of my heart I knew I had enough to give her. And as importantly, I had enough people around me to fill that reservoir back up so that I could do it all again tomorrow, next week, and next year.

And so I would.

We continued the therapy sessions moving from mad to bad. Victoria didn't suffer remorse. She also didn't have any cause-and-effect thinking. I would have to remind her when I asked her to do something that she had two options. She could do what I asked, be obedient, and feel good, or she could choose not to do it and receive a specific consequence.

Max had her name things from the past that she had done wrong. She had no problems coming up with a long list and a little too delightfully for me. Max asked her if she felt bad about any of the things she had listed. "No, not really. Except for stealing granola bars. I have stolen plenty of those," she too-proudly replied. She had made some progress. She had a few instances where I believed she was truly sorry. We just hadn't had enough of them. She hasn't been in a good place emotionally long enough to allow her to feel remorse.

One night as I cuddled with Victoria, she expressed true emotions as she began to talk about her discontent with herself. She burst into heavy, painful tears. It was no surprise that she had virtually no self-worth. And it didn't matter how much praise I gave her, if she didn't recognize it within herself, she would never believe it. She talked specifically about how she felt like junk, a piece of trash. She felt like she was bad. She didn't know why I would want her. "Why would you keep me?" she questioned. She exposed every bit of her broken self, not the victim in her that used those same words. I let her talk about it and then I read her a book. A book that brought her hope: *You Are Special* by Max Lucado.

*Victoria feels my love at times. I don't feel her's. Without that reciprocation, I lack motivation. She can't understand why I don't just give her away. Some days in times of despair, I don't either, but I know I won't because I would have already done it.*

The next day in therapy Max helped her go a step beyond what I could do, to encourage hope and feel good about herself. Her joy was overwhelming. Max tried to get her to talk about feeling sad and bad. She wouldn't even go there. She was not letting go of her good feeling. Max wisely allowed her to stay in this good place. I was at first irritated that we didn't get any "therapy" accomplished, but on the way home I realized she needed so many more of these good moments (and so did I) so that she would have the confidence to discover them within herself and not be dependent on us creating them for her.

Victoria got into the back seat of the car and kept repeating, "This is as happy as I could possibly be!" She couldn't imagine, in letting go of the anger and hurt, she increased her capacity to feel more joy. This was more than happiness. This was pure joy. It was deeper and took more work to acquire. On the way home we sang songs to each other. It was bonding. I was giving Victoria the time she needed to allow herself to safely feel and not have to push for it to be more than what it was. I was careful, which is what I should have been in the beginning if I had only known.

This is not specific just to Victoria. This is a universal truth. As we let go of things in our lives that hold us back, we receive the ability to accomplish the things we really want to do and to feel more deeply in our relationships with others. *Letting go and letting in.* I remember many times Max told me to just "let it go." I hoped I would never hear those three words again. It wasn't as easy as it sounded, especially when we're hanging on to hurt, worry, grief, anxiety, fear, or whatever it was. But I soon understood, not only would I hear those three words again; I would be living with them daily. And so it becomes a process of examining our hearts often and letting go of the things that are holding us back. It doesn't matter if you're eight or eighty.

We begged, pleaded, and encouraged Victoria to do the right thing, to allow herself to be happy. And then, one day, she did it! For five whole days. It caught me completely off guard. She followed all the rules and her happiness was genuine. Instead of being excited, I was tentative. I was encouraging but cautious. I didn't know what this meant. I knew better than to expect anything beyond the present, no matter how good she seemed.

She touched me often and I still wasn't comfortable with it. I was not quick to reciprocate her loving actions. My heart remembered what her seemingly loving actions meant before—nothing, they were empty. And although this looked different and was trying to feel different, I couldn't trust yet that there was really something pure and free there. But, I realized I could no longer try to find the sincerity in the positive. I just had to take it for what it was worth. I couldn't try to determine what was real.

For four years I had just wanted to make sense of Victoria, to be in control and to have her feel. I think I finally had a very good understanding of her. I was in control and she was starting to feel. I noticed that she didn't get so angry anymore. She didn't appear mad, she appeared hurt. I took no comfort in her hurting; I took an enormous amount of comfort in her expressing true emotion. That was brave.

I didn't feel as good as I had hoped or as good as I thought I should be feeling. It was my heart. Some things will never change. Trusting came more easily but it would, I imagine, always be difficult.

I was weak. I was frustrated at myself but I am what I am. She was doing so great. She was trying to be happy. This was what we had waited for. And my reaction? Skepticism. It protected me and hurt her. I really thought by now all the hard stuff would be over. I figured by now I could do whatever was required of me with essentially no effort. Yet, this continued to be very hard, because even though she had become so obedient, she was still very protective of herself. I had thought that as soon as she stopped pushing for so much control, the love would just fall right into place. It didn't.

And so, I beat myself up for two days because I couldn't get my heart to a place to trust in her happiness. And then the third day, I don't know what changed, but my heart opened to allow her in to stay for a moment. Not wallow. I loved the control I had in her room, in my arms. It was dif-

*Getting Victoria to let go is so difficult. I can pay to go to therapy and maybe have it happen. I can try at home and have the same odds. The difference is the emotional toll it takes on me. In therapy, I leave most of the work to Max, suffer some emotional effects, but reap the short-lived rewards (if there are any) for that day. At home, I fight with myself to become vulnerable, making the task harder than it should. I allow her in to release her sad or hurt or whatever emotion she is truly expressing and then she slips slowly away and leaves me wanting. I want her to be happy. I want her to love me. I want to be the source of her happiness and the motivation for her loving me. Right now I don't feel like I am either.*

ferent than in therapy where I felt obligated to let her take whatever she wanted from me and do with it what she chose. That felt intrusive. I talked to her about her feelings. I talked to her about what was making her feel happy. I asked her if she still had hurt in her heart.

"A little," she said about her birth mom. "Can we talk about it?" she asked. "Sure," I replied.

She told me how it hurt that her mom gave her up and put her in an orphanage. I talked to her about letting the hurt go. I talked to her about why it was hard for me to trust her. I cried as I told her about my hurt. She cried over the pain she caused, expressing real empathy.

I told Victoria, "I needed your birth mom to give you up because you were mine and I needed you here to help me."

"How could I help you when I was being mean to you?" she asked.

"You helped me be a better mom," I said. She didn't understand. I told her someday I would share the whole story.

I still didn't know what the breakthroughs and the bonding moments meant in terms of permanent change. I had allowed myself to feel hopeful beyond expectant. That was disappointing but I was careful and so willing to give this smart, courageous, loving girl every opportunity to prove herself in the loving arms of a mother that never gave up on her.

In cuddle time with Victoria, I often had her just be still. I wouldn't let her talk. She just looked into my eyes. As I returned her gaze I tried to be sensitive to her spirit because that was where the truth of her resided. Everything else, everything I could see, was a façade.

I tried to be sensitive to the truth of what she was. I sensed her goodness and her longing to feel peace. I began to understand what was at stake and how many people desired to see her heal. I reminded her of all the people who cared about her, helped her, and wanted see her get better. All of these people understood, possibly none more than me, the amount of good she had to offer. I promised her that she did have what it took to trust and obey. She could do it. She would do it. And as she did, she wouldn't even be able to contain the love as it flowed freely from her heart.

*"Only great sorrow or great joy can reveal your truth. If you would be revealed you must either dance naked in the sun, or carry your cross."*
—Gibran

In the beginning months of therapy, my lament was, "I just wish I would have known all of this in the beginning when we brought her home." I didn't know some of these things for sure, for a very long time. Max *tried* to tell me, I *tried* to believe him. It had taken me a while to get there, trudging along with my cross. I felt like it took me ten times longer than it should to understand Victoria's behaviors, twice that long to make progress within myself. I truly have had to live it to learn it. However, despite the pain, especially the unexpected pain that came from trusting sources, I could never wish I had known. Far too many truths have been revealed and I am beginning to feel the warmth of the sun.

About once a week or maybe every two weeks, the weight of Victoria would crash down on me. I allowed myself to ask, "What makes me think I have what it takes to do this for her when it seems so daunting?" When I had one person after another telling me, "I could never do what you do." I stood in the kitchen with a friend of mine discussing Victoria's behaviors. She looked at me and said, "I know, I know." I wondered how she could really know what I was talking about. She continued, "I know I could never do what you do." I found no solace in that, because some days I didn't think I could do it either. The thoughts didn't remain very long, but the feeling was heavy and discouraging. I had enough faith to pull me out of it; I guess I just didn't have enough faith to keep from going there. If I had to do this alone, I couldn't. I know because I had tried. I eventually had so many people supporting me. A few that I saw and many that I didn't. That support included Max. I continue to take all that I have learned in the exchanges with him and go and do better, because of him, I know better. And I hope somewhere along the journey, I helped him.

I once asked Victoria if she ever wondered how Max knew how to help her. "Yep, he took love lessons," she said.

"Oh really? Where did he learn those?" I eagerly asked.

"From his mom," she replied, like I should have already known. "That's where everyone learns love lessons."

What she didn't know was she had taught me more about love than most will ever feel or understand. This, from the same girl, who lacked the ability to accept or show love for most of her short life. This, from the same girl, who had broken my heart into pieces. Relentlessly.

I would think I was avoiding the heartbreak. I didn't think I was letting her, until one day I would see all the pieces lying around me. As I picked up each piece, it hurt all over again. I picked up the piece that felt like there was no progress; I picked up the piece that reminded me how lonely it could be; the piece that reminded me she didn't care; I picked up the piece that reminded me I wasn't doing enough; the piece that reproached I wasn't doing it right; the piece that affirmed we were not done yet; the piece that complained I'm tired; the piece that accused I made this take longer than it should; the piece that confirmed she still wasn't feeling my efforts; the piece that reputed someone else could do so much better.

Then, after I'd picked them up, alone, I found myself somehow whole again. My whole heart reminded me that there had been progress, just that it was inches when I wanted feet. It reminded me that I did have help if I was willing to trust it; that I had a sweet and special witness since Victoria can feel and reciprocate my love; that I was doing what I could, when I could; that my best was more than enough. It reminded me that I was in it for the long haul; that I knew where to get more strength; that I could not compare myself; that I kept giving in return for all the glimpses of wholeness. It assured me I had the only heart that could heal hers.

I struggled to stay consistent with myself, in the middle of all Victoria's and life's inconsistencies, and at the end of each day where we have been in complete harmony, I learned love lessons.

# CHAPTER 11

# *Sustaining Power*

*Living a life in a reality that most people don't know about is lonely. Living a life where emotions are fighting a daily battle and everything looks all right on the surface is lonely.*

Support while caring for a RAD child is crucial. Finding support is often complicated. I lacked support for so long because I didn't know what I needed. I couldn't explain what was wrong with Victoria. I unintentionally alienated and even lashed out occasionally at those that tried to understand. I remember one instance when the extended family had gotten together for dinner. Victoria had been wearing glasses and she was constantly rubbing them with spit. We finally stopped asking her to keep them clean and just left them dirty. Right before dinner started, my sister-in-law Melinda asked, "Why don't you keep Victoria's glasses clean?"

That was a fair enough question, but she didn't know what a source of contention the glasses had been for us over the past months. And this was just one instance of many where Victoria drew attention to herself over controlling behaviors at home. Instead of directing the question back onto Victoria, I reacted with a disgusted, "Ugh!" because I didn't want to have to try to explain it and mostly because Victoria was getting the negative attention she was looking for. My sister-in-law responded, "Oh now we can't even talk about her glasses."

"No you can't," I defensively replied.

I knew it was reactionary the moment I said it, but the pressure I was under, especially at family events, and the misunderstanding that surrounded me, made me feel like I couldn't ever help them understand. I spent many family gatherings asking people not to talk to or pay any attention to Victoria. While this was helpful to me, it was damaging for

Victoria and those around her. It increased Victoria's anxiety and it made those around her feel very uncomfortable and uncertain. By the time I could explain Victoria's behaviors, I felt like I had already burned many bridges. I didn't know if anything I could say would help others understand what I was contending with or how it was actually helping Victoria heal. I didn't have all the answers but I did have a greater understanding of RAD, and most importantly, I had my intuition. I think it's very important for parents to have a strong foundation of knowledge so they can feel confident; not only implementing techniques they believe will help their children but feel self-assured in explaining it to others, even when others don't understand it. Now when we are at family gatherings, I take something for Victoria to do and she stays next to me. Occasionally, if I think she can handle it, I may play a card game with her and have a couple of other people play with us. As soon as she can appreciate and really want to be a part of her own family, she can start interacting with extended family members.

My circle of support in the beginning was limited by choice and circumstance. I had a hard time following Max's fourth rule: Ask for help. Initially I found it very difficult to reveal my deepest hurt safely, especially when I didn't fully understand Victoria or myself. Max encouraged me to call other mothers with RAD children. I couldn't bring myself to do it, because I didn't believe they would be able to understand my torment. I wanted to be so independent and was reluctant to feel needy.

I wanted those closest to me to help but either they couldn't understand, frustrated me, or only tried to fix. Everyone seemed to have great ideas—from loving her more to getting her more involved in activities. The best support was from Jay, Max, and a few people who "got it." I loved to talk to others who had no idea what RAD was. I got Victoria's story down to a short compelling version. I don't know if it was my intensity or their interest that kept them asking questions. I was able to educate others about RAD and also see similarities in non-RAD children. This was the most therapeutic thing for me—sharing my story, my insight, and finding parallels in others' children even if not exactly the same, because Victoria's actions came from a very different kind of thought process. I found encouragement from those who listened to my heartache, who were genuinely interested, and asked questions. Eventually when I gained a better base of knowledge about RAD, (which increased my confidence), I began to reach out to other parents, especially mothers. And I realized we don't have to have the same experiences to offer empathy and support. I believe it doesn't matter how a child is reacting—to a mother's heart it feels the same.

The reasons why children have disrupted attachments isn't confusing, but I think the coping mechanisms the children use are hard for people to comprehend. And also, the techniques used to treat Victoria were unusual. No one could understand the matter-of- fact approach we had with her. It did look strict and unnatural from the outside, but we weren't dealing with a normal kid. Her thought process was crazy-making and we had to respond creatively. And sometimes it still feels crazy to me. It's true those looking in thought we were punishing Victoria all day long for breaking a rule in the morning. But what they couldn't see was her frame of mind. For example, one morning I wouldn't let her go out with her Grandparents, then that afternoon her brother was in charge of her and had sent her to her room. And later, when I fed her dinner, I forgot to give her a drink. What I didn't realize and she didn't express was that her anger was escalating. But you couldn't see it from the smile on her face. That was why it didn't take much to set her off. She had accumulated so much anger all day long and she could have hung onto it all week long. She would continue to make me pay for injustices she thought she received. Most of the time she was holding onto grudges. I forget to give her a drink. Mad at Mom, mean all day. No cuddle time at therapy. Mad at Mom, mean all week. Many times what was making her angry came from really innocent actions on our part but I couldn't make the connections and she wouldn't tell us. But she would push us.

As we implemented the techniques in the beginning of therapy, Victoria began to push harder against me. It was vital that I found people that could provide me respite from Victoria. I recognized quickly that most people I knew wouldn't be able to do the things I requested from them while she was in their care. When she went over to someone's house, it wasn't playtime. They would need to give Victoria a chore to do. They couldn't give her treats or let her ask for anything. They couldn't give her any physical affection or be endearing. Victoria was always looking for a reason to live at someone else's house. She spent so much time pushing us away from her that if she received food, affection, and attention from others, it prolonged her healing and set us back.

"It's okay." I heard that twice in one day from people that knew my situation very well. I was talking to my mom.

"How is school going for Victoria?"

"Well," I said, "she hates it and she hates me."

"Oh well, that's okay."

Huh? What part of her hating me am I ever suppose to be okay with? I never will be.

I then pick her up from the center we enrolled her in that catered especially to controlling children. I tell her teacher, "It is frustrating and sad that she had made progress over the summer and I began to see her for who she really is and sense sincere emotion. Now, school has set her back and now I see emptiness—a lack of emotion and motivation."

"That's okay," she said.

So I reply the same way I did to my mother. "No, it isn't okay."

Did I have to accept it? Sure. Did I have to keep helping her in spite of her? Absolutely. But did I have to be okay with it? No, I didn't. And I wasn't because she had allowed herself to trust me, which told me she was capable of forming an attachment.

One of the most important things that sustained me daily was the pure love my boys freely gave me. They probably won't ever understand how in taking my love, appreciating it, and returning theirs', they made life bearable for me.

One day I was sitting on the couch reading a book to Noah. He was cuddled up at my side and I was feeling every bit of his love for me and mine for him. Grant walked into the room as we were finishing and looked like he needed some attention as well. I called him over and told him to come sit by me. He looked at Noah and said, "Why does he get the best seat in the house again?" Tender mercies. I lifted Noah to the other side of me. I then had them both snuggled close to me, feeling twice as much love. After finishing, they left and I called Victoria over. She then took the best seat in the house. But something was very different. I wasn't really thinking or feeling anything when all of the sudden a big, dull, ache resonated from the center of my chest. I know I had felt heartache before, but this was the first time I could recall that it was not only so strong but the only thing I could feel at that moment. It put the pain I feel, from what she doesn't, in total perspective. I don't allow myself to experience it very often or it would become overwhelming and discouraging.

Sometimes I questioned all the effort when I didn't feel like there was much progress. I wondered if it was me more than her? If I didn't feel like giving up, I felt like giving in and some days I did. I would just let Victoria make her own choices and do what she wanted, within reason, treating her like her brothers, which was what so many people pressured me to do. And I would pay for it. She would begin to feel more entitled, aggravate her brothers, and continue to sneak and steal things out of bedrooms and the pantry. She couldn't handle the responsibility, focus, or make good decisions. It never lasted more than a couple of days before Jay and the boys insisted she return to some structure and consistency. And I knew it too but I think part of me so badly wanted her to be ready. I longed for her to be able to settle and think clearly. I wanted to send her to friends' houses, enroll her in dance lessons, and let her spend a week at her grandparents' house. I wanted her to be able to play at home and be creative and loving, not manipulating and mean. But she wasn't ready and every now and then I needed to see that and have a small reprieve. But it would set her back. As I became more comfortable with what I was doing for Victoria and gained better insight into her, I began to stay the course. I didn't let up and I could see progress. When someone would ask me how Victoria was doing, I had to look at the past six months and not the past six days to see that she was healing.

It's all about perspective with RAD children, and few people have the vantage point that parents do. The best support one can offer a parent of a RAD child is encouragement and trust. I remember so clearly the phone call from my mom four years after Victoria's arrival home when she said, "Jodi, I don't understand everything you do with Victoria, but I want you to know that I believe you have been doing everything right." I didn't necessarily need her to believe I was doing everything right since it wasn't exactly true, but I did need to know she trusted me to know what was best for Victoria. It helped that my mom spent time learning and educating herself about RAD. I didn't need her to have all the answers for Victoria. I needed her supportive love and trust in me.

The journey to healing a RAD child is exhausting. It can be full of second-guessing, frustration, disappointment, and sadness. It can also be full of hope, strength, determination, and success. It does require that we have support. A therapist that understands attachment disorder; friends and family who are willing to trust in things they don't completely understand; husbands who are willing to be on the same page so the RAD child can't divide and conquer; mothers that will take the time to care for themselves so they can care for others and have confidence in ourselves.

# CHAPTER 12

# *Lessons Learned*

*Opening up, letting in, letting go, letting trust, letting sad,
letting hurt, letting it all feel okay. I feel tentative.
I feel restrained. I don't know if it's my wall or my will.*

My journey with Victoria has taught me many things about myself, emotions, and complicated human relationships. I have often reflected on why I have never read my story anywhere. The answer is simple: because it's only now being written. It is now clear that bringing Victoria and me together with our individual mechanisms for survival was a recipe for disaster. We both demanded control. We were stuck in a stalemate. I couldn't just "live with it." It is this aspect of our relationship that I think made things so unique and complicated.

I didn't mean for my torment to be so visible and obvious, but for so long, I lived in ignorance trying to pretend everything was all right, and that was so destructive. I don't think my trial with Victoria was any worse or more complicated than what others will struggle with in their lives. I know we will all face challenges. It could easily include finding ourselves loving under the most difficult of circumstances. Trying to love someone who has no interest in loving in return is heart-wrenching, but I do think that despite my early weaknesses, I exerted an enormous amount of strength to not only battle Victoria's demons but mine as well. I knew there was a serious problem. I sought help and I did what needed to be done to fix what was broken. I take satisfaction in knowing that despite how inundated I felt, I had the fortitude to do something about it. I wasn't willing to live with the anger and indifference Victoria had for me. I couldn't.

So I try not to be so reactionary to those around me, but I am also not willing to change how I am raising Victoria based on other people's skepticism or their misunderstanding. I will have to risk being alienated while I think I am doing what is best for my daughter even if others aren't comfortable with it.

I still have to be ready whenever she is willing—it doesn't feel as manipulative now, as I just try to capture those brief periods of trusting as opportunities to reinforce my love for her. I know enough of those periods will become permanent. I just don't know when. I have finally stopped asking Max. He really doesn't know. He can't.

I used to think that if I could just be more of everything, Victoria would be everything she needed to be. If she was doing most things right, why wasn't I feeling better about the relationship? Why weren't we having amazing moments creating lasting memories? It must be me. It wasn't. I have to remind myself of this often. I try to reassure her I have everything she needs. As she trusts in me she will begin to get what she wants. Her heart is not yet convinced. Right now her obedience is predicated on what is in it for her. That is why even though she is doing most things right I still find it hard to trust her. But I'll take it. Because I know my consistent, careful, and creative love balanced with structure and accountability will someday allow us to trust each other freely. Finding and keeping the balance is a work in progress and is hard to maintain.

I've also convinced myself that this is my journey. I don't need to feel or look like any other mother. My strengths and weaknesses are specific to me. I try to appreciate the things I do well and recognize my weaknesses as a part of me to work on making stronger.

I can't compare myself, try to be different, or more than I am. I must be gentle with myself. But I must keep trying to do better, especially because I know better. And that is why sometimes uncovering the truth is harder than the unknown, because it requires something from us. But truth also gives us something in return—enlightenment, direction, comfort, and confidence. Truth sets us free.

I have felt naïve and ignorant. Is this a typical discovery of moms with RAD kids? Or is it just my story? I don't ever read about moms being as angry as I was. They are always just trying to do what is best for the child or at least that's what they say. Where is the cycle of intense love to intense hate to intense indifference? During these times, not only did I not know what was best for Victoria, I eventually didn't want the best for her. I am not proud of how I handled Victoria in the beginning, I am profoundly sorry and humbled, but am I so unique? Am I the only one with unresolved hurt that catapulted me into chaos? Am I the only one that continued to take things personally for so long? Am I the only one weak enough to think a five-year-old could intentionally victimize me? Am I the only one that was pushed to the edge of insanity because I couldn't make sense of her or eventually myself? For a very long time, I did feel like the only one.

So while life is still a rollercoaster, there is forward momentum. Victoria has begun to trust. Occasionally she throws up her wall faster than I can stop her and it does set us back a bit. But we work together and again get beyond the fortress. It is a cycle and I can see her healing.

During the first few years I really thought this was something Victoria would grow out of with maturity. However, four years later I see this will never happen. Her maturity will continue to struggle and she will just find different ways to fulfill needs she doesn't trust me to meet. That is scary because I know as she gets older her choices for ways to meet needs will grow more dangerous.

Victoria's obsession with relying on others to make her feel good is frightening. This is the stuff addictions are made of. This isn't a typical kid's demand for being entertained. She wants to be having fun all the time and when she isn't, she is angry. When she is angry, she begins to live in this dangerous fantasyland and wants to hold someone responsible for not providing constant attention or happiness. That would be mostly me. This dangerous fantasyland conjures up all kinds of half-truths, total delusion, and vindictiveness. Her view of reality is distorted by what she has lived and how she really wants to be living but her mind, so abused by her past, will not allow her to think clearly. Between trying to say the right thing and suppressing her true feelings, she is caught in the abyss.

Time would have just made things worse for her. Finding help early was the answer. Finding help with a qualified attachment therapist, supportive schoolteachers, and supportive friends easily was a challenge.

I know that this takes perseverance. I know this takes an enormous amount of support. I know that much of the support I receive must come from within because depending on encouragement outside of me is often frustrating and disappointing. My strength from within is born of my hope from above. I don't know how to survive this type of emotional turmoil without relying on a higher source.

Before Victoria's arrival into my life, I found it difficult to express my deepest emotions, especially my hurt. I lived looking like everything was great on the outside; anything less would have left me vulnerable and weak, so I thought. At times when I couldn't contain my hurt and allowed it to show, it had to be short-lived. I'd pull it together and move on.

I'm still not comfortable laying my heartache and shortcomings on the line for all to see, but I've learned, especially from Victoria, especially from being me that hanging onto the hurt with a smile on my face doesn't help, it hinders.

As I've discovered who Victoria really is, I've discovered who I really am. And one thing I know for sure is I am the best mom for Victoria. And I love her.

The letter in the beginning of the book was written when I first went to meet Max after stopping therapy for Victoria. Typically, writing letters, even letters you never intend to send, is very healing. Max wasn't specific; he simply told me to write a letter to Victoria. I didn't want to do it, but I did. My letter first started out soft and gentle, but nothing was coming out on paper. So, I wrote what I had really felt the first couple of years with Victoria in our home and that letter was the outcome. But healing was nowhere to be found. I had written it late at night. I read the letter to my husband and his head nodded in agreement as I read. I was amazed I could write down my feelings so specifically. I fell right to sleep, but my nightmare started when I woke up. The minute I opened my eyes I couldn't stop thinking of the letter. I felt like that angry mom who was so bad. The trauma encompassed me and sent me right back to the anxiety filled days. My heart was racing, my breath was shallow, and I couldn't move. I just lay there and cried. I wondered "If I had really repented of the things I had done, how could I still feel like this reckless woman?" The answer was Post Traumatic Stress Syndrome. I sent Max a text notifying him that something with this healing exercise had gone tragically wrong. He couldn't have known but he did get me in his office quickly to calm my fears. He asked me to read the letter to him. I fought it. I didn't want him to know these things about me. "I'm not bad," I kept telling him. "I know," he replied. But I didn't believe him. I finally read the letter and couldn't deny it was all me, and it was all true. We did some EMDR exercises which focuses on relaxation and processing traumatic events. I was skeptical, but I was also desperate. I tried to cooperate in the eye movement, blinking, and breathing. And it worked. I did feel relaxed and I was able to read the letter calmly before I left. Max made some suggestions as to what to do with the letter: I could burn it; mail it to myself; or throw it away on the way out of his office. But I knew I would keep it. I knew that even though I wasn't proud of the woman that wrote it, the feelings were real and other mothers would be able to relate. It was also important as it helped begin my journey to opening up and allowing Max to help me. And it made me relieved, grateful ,and ultimately able to write:


Dear Victoria,

It has been a very long, tiring, confusing three-and-a-half years. I am sorry that I had so many lessons to learn at your expense. I am sorry I wasn't prepared for you. I am sorry that I allowed my past to dictate my reactions to you. I know who you saw wasn't who I really am. I am sorry that's the only Mom you've ever known.

I was reacting. I honestly didn't know what was causing the intensity, but worse, I didn't know how to stop it. Not only could I not make sense of you, I didn't know what was going on with myself.

Victoria, you are selfish and manipulative but that does not justify one act of unkindness or indifference from me. We still have a bit of a journey ahead of us. I can't promise you that I won't get frustrated, disappointed, or impatient; but what I can promise you is respect and love that you so deserve from a mother who has enough love for you and is no longer buried by fear, contempt, or helplessness.

I don't know how much more heartache or exhaustion lay ahead for me. But this I do know—I can do whatever is required of me because I have all the help I need this time. I know that I am the only one who can do this for you, and I will. I know I want you to be free of the fear, anxiety, and sadness that dominates your countenance. I am ready this time. All of me.

—Love, Mom (finally forgiving myself)

# *Epilogue*

$\mathcal{W}$ill she ever heal? That is my most constant question. Victoria is healing. There isn't much more I can do for her but love her, help her feel safe in structure and predictability, and then it is up to her to do the rest. This is now the hardest part: acceptance, knowing I am doing everything I can even if she gets stuck or quits. I can't make her want more or want me. I can use discipline and privileges to motivate but eventually she needs to do the right things for the right reasons. And I believe she will. She has every opportunity afforded to her to help develop and maintain meaningful emotional attachments. But it will be up to her. And right now we cycle. It's frustrating and it does hurt to watch her fall.

Each time she has good days they usually last longer and feel better than the previous stretch because we are building upon the trust that allows her to let go of the fear. Her willingness to obey seems predicated more on feeling good now than fearing a consequence. She is more comfortable being in my arms and looks less nervous and uncertain. She opens up more easily and is more truthful. And while her bad days are getting shorter they do seem worse, because she has further to fall and it hurts me more because I get pushed further away. I no longer cycle with her up and down. She doesn't come crashing in on me every few weeks. I fight the self-doubt and maintain confidence in myself. There is so much comfort in knowing I am now able and willing to do all I can for her no matter what she chooses to do with my love and support. But it is still and will always be emotionally taxing and physically demanding. I can't get away from that.

I continue to learn and discover new ways to help Victoria, which right now include occasional play therapy, therapeutic horseback riding, working with Max, and (mostly) my intuition. She attends a center that maintains the boundaries and consistency she receives at home. It's just a matter of staying the course and being aware of the opportunities to help her heal.

Jay and I are continually attentive to the boys, although we don't know the full impact growing up with Victoria has had on their lives. We do our best to create opportunities for them to express their feelings and increase their understanding of Victoria's atypical behaviors. We find time to do things with them without Victoria and all of her distractions and to strengthen our bonds with each other. Recently we left her in respite (someone who understands RAD) while the family went out of town. I remember the first day waking up and feeling so much relief that she wasn't there because she takes so much work. But soon tears began to stream down my face because I missed her being a part of the family, making memories, and building relationships. I asked Noah a few days later, "Do you miss Victoria?"

And he answered quickly, "I do, but I don't know why." I hugged him and told him I knew exactly what he was feeling.

I can sense the boys want to give her chances and are waiting for the opportunity to be more involved in her life. I also know this experience has increased their patience, empathy, desire to do the right thing, and pulled us closer together as a family. It could have had the opposite effect but instead it's teaching them love lessons. Victoria is teaching us all love lessons.

# Favorite Cuddletime Book List

*The Kissing Hand,* **Audrey Penn,** Tanglewood Press 2006

*Love is a Handful of Honey,* **Giles Andreae,** Orchard Books 2001

*Just in Case You Ever Wonder,* **Max Lucado,** Thomas Nelson 2007

*You Are Special,* **Max Lucado,** Crossway Books 2007

*The Little Soul and the Sun,* **Neale Donald Walsch,** Hampton Rd Pub Co 1998

*You Are My I Love You,* **Maryann Cusimano,** Philomel 2001

*Hope Is An Open Heart,* **Lauren Thompson,** Scholastic Press 2008

*I'll Love You Forever,* Robert M Munsch and Sheila McGraw, Firefly Books 1995

# Books on Attachment

*Attachment, Trauma, and Healing: Understanding and Treating Attachment Disorder in Children,* **Terry M. Levy and Michael Orlans,** CWLA Press, 1998

*Healing Parents: Helping Wounded Children Learn to Trust and Love,* **Micheal Orlans and Terry M. Levy,** CWLA Press 2006

*Parenting with Love and Logic,* **Foster Kline and Jim Fay,** NavPress Pub 2006

*New Families, Old Scripts: A Guide to the Language of Trauma and Attachment in Adoptive Families,* **Carolyn Archer,** Jessica Kingsley Publishers 2006

*When Love Is Not Enough: A Guide to Parenting Children with RAD,* **Nancy Thomas,** Families By Design 2005